AI Trading Agents: Build Autonomous Systems for Stock Market Analysis and Execution

Reid Thornton

AI TRADING AGENTS: BUILD AUTONOMOUS SYSTEMS FOR STOCK MARKET ANALYSIS AND EXECUTION

First edition. March 12, 2026.

ISBN: 979-8233044007

Written by Reid Thornton.

Table of Contents

Why I Let Machines Trade for Me (and Why You Might Want To)

I didn't start out wanting to build AI trading agents.

I started out wanting to not stare at charts at 2:47 a.m., convincing myself that this time the breakout was "different." I wanted fewer emotional decisions, fewer impulsive trades, and far fewer moments where I asked myself why I trusted a single candlestick more than basic probability.

Like a lot of traders, I tried everything first. Indicators stacked on indicators. Strategies that worked beautifully for three months and then died without warning. Backtests that looked like money-printing machines until they met the real market and immediately fell apart. The problem wasn't intelligence or effort. The problem was that markets don't reward hope, vibes, or heroic intuition. They reward systems.

That realization is what led me down the rabbit hole of AI trading agents.

Not bots that blindly follow rules. Not black boxes you pray over before hitting "deploy." But autonomous systems that observe markets, learn from data, adapt to changing conditions, manage risk, and execute trades without panic or ego. Systems that do exactly what they're designed to do—and nothing more.

This book is the result of that journey. It's the book I wish I had before I burned countless hours reinventing wheels, trusting bad backtests, and learning market lessons the expensive way.

And no, this isn't a "get rich quick" story. It's a "build something that survives" story.

What This Book Is Really About

At its core, this book is about decision-making under uncertainty. Trading just happens to be the most honest environment to test it. Markets don't care about your confidence. They don't care about your degree. They don't even care if your model is elegant. They only care whether your system can consistently make better decisions than randomness after costs.

So we focus on building agents that can do exactly that.

We start with how markets work, because ignoring market structure is how most strategies die early. Then we move into data—the good, the bad, and the completely misleading. From there, we build up machine learning foundations, layer in deep learning and reinforcement learning, and eventually arrive at full autonomous agents that can trade, manage risk, and adapt without human babysitting.

Along the way, I'll point out where things usually break. Because they will break. That's normal. The goal isn't perfection. The goal is resilience.

What You'll Learn

Introduction to AI Trading Agents

We kick things off by defining what an AI trading agent actually is—and what it is not. You'll learn why most "AI trading bots" aren't really AI at all, and why autonomy matters more than prediction accuracy.

Financial Markets and Trading Fundamentals

Before building agents, you need to understand the battlefield. This chapter covers market structure, instruments, order types, liquidity, and why ignoring execution details can quietly destroy an otherwise solid strategy.

Data Sources for AI Trading Systems

Data is fuel, and bad data is poison. We walk through market data, alternative data, and the hidden biases that sneak into datasets and sabotage models before they ever go live.

Data Engineering and Feature Construction

This is where raw data turns into signals. You'll learn how to clean, align, transform, and engineer features that actually carry information instead of noise.

Machine Learning Foundations for Trading

We cover supervised and unsupervised learning with a trading-first mindset. No academic detours—just what works, what doesn't, and how to evaluate models in a non-stationary world.

Deep Learning Models in Trading

Neural networks, CNNs, transformers—powerful tools that are also very good at overfitting. You'll learn when deep learning helps, when it hurts, and how to keep models grounded in reality.

Reinforcement Learning for Trading Agents

This is where agents start making decisions instead of predictions. We break down environments, rewards, policies, and why reinforcement learning is both exciting and incredibly easy to misuse in markets.

Agent Architectures and System Design

Trading agents don't live in notebooks forever. This chapter shows how to design modular, scalable agent architectures that can evolve without collapsing under their own complexity.

Strategy Design and Signal Generation

Alpha doesn't magically appear. You'll learn structured approaches to hypothesis testing, signal combination, and building strategies that adapt when regimes change.

Risk Management and Position Sizing

If this chapter feels boring, it means you haven't blown up yet. We cover volatility, drawdowns, capital allocation, and how agents should think about risk before thinking about returns.

Execution Algorithms and Market Impact

Execution is where paper profits go to die. This chapter focuses on slippage, transaction costs, and how intelligent execution can matter more than signal quality.

Backtesting and Simulation Frameworks

Backtests lie unless you force them not to. You'll learn how to build realistic simulations, avoid common traps, and stress-test agents before they touch real capital.

Evaluation and Performance Attribution

When things go wrong—and they will—you need to know why. This chapter covers attribution, diagnostics, and detecting strategy decay before it becomes catastrophic.

Deployment and Infrastructure

From local experiments to live systems. We discuss architecture, latency, reliability, monitoring, and what it actually takes to run agents in production.

Governance, Compliance, and Ethics

Just because you can automate something doesn't mean you should blindly. We explore regulation, transparency, and responsible use of autonomous trading systems.

Maintaining and Evolving Trading Agents

Markets change. Agents must change faster. This chapter focuses on retraining, adaptation, debugging live systems, and surviving regime shifts.

Future Directions in AI Trading

Multi-agent systems, self-improving models, and where humans still matter. We wrap up by looking ahead—and grounding expectations firmly in reality.

What You'll Walk Away With

By the end of this book, you won't just understand AI trading agents—you'll think like one.

You'll know how to turn messy market data into usable signals. How to design agents that make decisions instead of guesses. How to manage risk systematically. How to test ideas without lying to yourself. And how to deploy systems that don't crumble the moment conditions change.

Most importantly, you'll stop looking for perfect strategies and start building robust systems.

And if, somewhere along the way, you also get a little more sleep and a lot fewer emotional trades, I'd call that a win.

Chapter 1: Introduction to AI Trading Agents

I didn't wake up one day and say, "You know what sounds fun? Let's give machines access to financial markets." This chapter exists because humans are emotional, inconsistent, and wildly overconfident—especially when money is involved. I've made trades based on vibes, caffeine levels, and the assumption that "it has to bounce eventually." Spoiler: it didn't. That's where trading agents enter the story.

This chapter introduces the concept of AI trading agents, explains how they differ from traditional algorithms, and outlines the benefits and risks of autonomy in financial markets. It sets expectations for what agents can and cannot do while framing the system-oriented mindset used throughout the book.

1.1 Evolution of Algorithmic and AI-Driven Trading

Algorithmic trading did not appear fully formed with neural networks and GPUs. It evolved through very practical needs: execute faster, remove human error, reduce costs, and scale decision-making. Understanding this evolution matters because most failures in modern AI trading come from misunderstanding which problems machines were actually built to solve—and which ones they still struggle with.

This section walks through that evolution in four practical phases, focusing on what changed technically, what worked, and what still applies today.

Phase 1: Rule-Based Automation (1980s–1990s)

The earliest trading algorithms were not intelligent. They were automation scripts.

- Problem being solved
- Humans were slow at execution
- Manual trading introduced errors
- Institutions needed consistency at scale

What systems looked like

- Hard-coded rules
- Deterministic logic
- No learning, no adaptation

Example logic:

- Buy if price crosses above a moving average
- Sell if position loses more than X%
- Execute VWAP over the trading day

Practical takeaway

Rule-based systems worked best when:

- Market structure was stable
- Latency advantages mattered
- The goal was execution efficiency, not prediction

Many modern systems still rely on this logic—for execution, risk limits, and fail-safes. These components should never be "learned." They should be enforced.

Phase 2: Statistical Arbitrage and Optimization (1990s–2000s)

As computing power increased, firms moved from fixed rules to statistical relationships.

What changed

- Strategies became data-driven
- Decisions were based on probability, not certainty
- Optimization entered the loop

Common techniques:

- Linear regression
- Cointegration
- Mean reversion models
- Portfolio optimization

Typical workflow

- Identify a statistical relationship
- Estimate parameters from historical data
- Trade deviations
- Rebalance periodically

Failure mode

Most strategies died not because the math was wrong, but because:

- Transaction costs were underestimated
- Relationships decayed
- Models assumed stationarity

Practical takeaway

Statistical models introduced rigor, but they were still:

- Static
- Re-trained infrequently

- Blind to regime shifts

This limitation directly led to machine learning adoption.

Phase 3: Machine Learning for Prediction (2000s–2010s)

Machine learning entered trading to solve one problem:

markets are nonlinear and unstable.

Instead of hand-designing relationships, practitioners let models infer them.

What ML actually improved

- Feature interactions
- Nonlinear patterns
- High-dimensional data handling

Common models:

- Tree-based methods (Random Forests, Gradient Boosting)
- Support Vector Machines
- Shallow neural networks

Typical use

ML was mostly used for prediction, not decision-making:

- Predict returns
- Predict direction
- Predict volatility
- Generate signals

Then humans or rule engines handled:

- Position sizing
- Risk
- Execution

Key insight

High predictive accuracy did not guarantee profitability.

Many models failed because:

- Targets were poorly defined
- Labels leaked future information
- Small improvements didn't survive costs

Practical takeaway

Prediction alone is insufficient. Trading performance depends on how predictions are used, not how accurate they look.

This gap led directly to agent-based systems.

Phase 4: AI Trading Agents (2010s–Present)

AI trading agents shift the framing entirely.

Instead of asking:

- *"Can we predict the market?"*

They ask:

- *"What action should the system take now, given its objectives and constraints?"*

What defines an agent

An agent:

- Observes the environment
- Takes actions
- Receives feedback
- Updates behavior over time

This includes:

- Reinforcement learning agents
- Multi-agent systems
- Hybrid ML + rules systems

Why this matters

Markets are not prediction problems. They are decision problems under uncertainty.

Agents allow:

- Direct optimization of trading outcomes
- End-to-end learning (state → action → reward)
- Adaptation to changing conditions

Example: prediction vs agent

Prediction-based:

- Model forecasts +0.3% return
- Rule engine decides position size
- Risk layer may override decision

Agent-based:

- State includes price, inventory, volatility, costs
- Agent decides buy, sell, hold, or do nothing
- Reward reflects PnL, risk, and costs directly

Minimal Agent Loop (Conceptual)

This is the core loop every trading agent eventually implements, regardless of complexity:

while market_is_open:

state = observe_market()

action = policy(state)

execute(action)

reward = calculate_reward()

update_policy(state, action, reward)

Everything else—deep learning, transformers, ensembles—is just machinery around this loop.

What Actually Improved Over Time

Despite the hype, progress has been incremental, not revolutionary.

What genuinely improved:

- Data availability
- Latency and infrastructure
- Feature richness

- Simulation realism

What did not magically improve:

- Market predictability
- Stability of alpha
- Robustness under regime shifts

Important reality

Most profitable systems today are:

- Hybrid
- Constraint-heavy
- Conservative in learning
- Aggressive in risk control

Purely autonomous, unconstrained agents are rare—and usually short-lived.

Why This History Matters for You

If you skip this evolution, you'll repeat old mistakes with new tools.

Common modern errors:

- Using deep learning where rules are better
- Letting agents learn risk constraints
- Optimizing rewards disconnected from real costs
- Assuming more data equals more edge

Design principle to carry forward

- Automate execution early
- Learn signals cautiously
- Enforce risk mechanically
- Allow autonomy only where feedback is reliable

That philosophy underpins every chapter that follows.

AI trading agents are not smarter traders.

They are systems that make fewer emotional mistakes—when designed correctly.

1.2 What Makes an Agent Autonomous

There is a difference between a trading system and a trading agent. Many systems execute trades automatically. Very few are truly autonomous.

Autonomy is not about using machine learning. It is not about complexity. It is about independent decision-making under uncertainty with minimal human intervention.

If you remove yourself from the loop during market hours and the system can still operate safely, adapt to conditions, and manage risk within defined constraints—that is autonomy.

This section breaks down what actually makes a trading agent autonomous in practice.

1. Perception: Continuous Environmental Awareness

An autonomous agent must observe the market in structured form.

This includes:

- Price and volume
- Order book state
- Volatility regime
- Position exposure
- Realized and unrealized PnL
- Risk limits

The key distinction:

- A rule-based system reacts to single signals.
- An autonomous agent interprets state.

State is a structured representation of everything relevant at a decision point.

Example state structure in Python:

state = {

"mid_price": mid_price,

"volatility": realized_vol,

"order_imbalance": imbalance,

"inventory": current_position,

"cash": available_capital,

"drawdown": current_drawdown

}

Autonomy begins when decisions are conditioned on context, not isolated indicators.

2. Decision Authority: Action Selection Without Manual Approval

Many trading systems generate signals but still rely on:

- Human confirmation
- Manual sizing
- External override logic

An autonomous agent:

- Chooses action
- Determines position size
- Executes without approval
- Operates within predefined constraints

Actions typically include:

- Buy
- Sell
- Hold
- Reduce exposure
- Flatten position

In reinforcement learning terms:

action = policy(state)

The policy may be:

- A neural network
- A probabilistic model
- A rule-augmented model

The defining characteristic is not how the action is computed, but that it is self-selected in real time.

3. Feedback Integration: Learning or Adaptive Behavior

A system that never changes is automated.

A system that updates behavior based on outcomes is autonomous.

Feedback can be implemented in several ways:

Static Autonomy (Limited Adaptation)

- Model retrained daily or weekly
- Parameters adjusted offline
- Execution behavior adaptive but strategy fixed

Dynamic Autonomy (Online Adaptation)

- Policy updated continuously
- Risk adjusted based on volatility
- Position sizing reacts to drawdown
- Regime detection modifies strategy weights

Example adaptive sizing rule:

if volatility > threshold:

*position_size *= 0.5*

This is simple, but it reflects adaptive behavior.

True autonomy requires at least some mechanism that allows the system to respond to changing market structure.

4. Constraint Awareness: Operating Within Boundaries

Autonomy without constraints is dangerous.

An autonomous trading agent must operate within hard-coded limits:

- Max position size
- Max daily loss
- Max leverage
- Exposure limits per asset
- Kill-switch triggers

These are not optional. They are enforced guardrails.

Example:

if daily_loss > max_daily_loss:

close_all_positions()

disable_trading()

Important distinction:

Risk limits should not be learned. They should be enforced mechanically.

Autonomy exists inside constraints, not beyond them.

5. Objective Alignment: Reward Reflects Real Goals

An agent is autonomous only if it optimizes the correct objective.

Poor reward design creates destructive autonomy.

Bad reward examples:

- Rewarding raw returns without cost
- Ignoring slippage
- Ignoring drawdowns
- Ignoring tail risk

Better reward example:

reward = pnl - transaction_cost - risk_penalty

Where risk penalty could include:

- Volatility scaling
- Drawdown penalty
- Inventory cost

If the objective is wrong, the agent will behave "rationally" in the wrong direction.

Autonomy amplifies reward design errors.

6. Persistence: Operating Without Continuous Supervision

A backtest can look autonomous. It is not.

Real autonomy is tested when:

- Markets gap unexpectedly
- Liquidity disappears
- Data feeds break
- Latency spikes

An autonomous agent must handle:

- Missing data
- Execution rejections
- Partial fills
- Connectivity failures

Basic resilience example:

try:

execute_order(order)

except ExecutionError:

retry_with_smaller_size()

Robustness is a defining feature of autonomy.

7. Degrees of Autonomy

Autonomy is not binary. It exists on a spectrum.

- **Level 0** – Signal generator only
- **Level 1** – Automated execution
- **Level 2** – Automated decision + fixed sizing
- **Level 3** – Adaptive sizing and regime response
- **Level 4** – Learning-based policy optimization
- **Level 5** – Multi-agent coordination with dynamic objective adjustment

Most profitable production systems operate between Level 2 and Level 4.

Fully unconstrained Level 5 autonomy is rare outside research environments.

What Autonomy Is Not

It is not:

- Using deep learning
- Running on GPUs
- Being complex
- Trading frequently
- Being fully unsupervised

Some of the most autonomous systems are structurally simple but:

- Context-aware
- Self-sizing
- Risk-controlled
- Adaptive to volatility

Complexity does not equal autonomy.

Practical Checklist for Building Autonomy

Before calling your system autonomous, verify:

- Does it define state explicitly?
- Does it choose actions without human approval?
- Does it adjust behavior based on feedback?
- Are hard risk constraints enforced mechanically?
- Is the reward aligned with real economic outcomes?
- Can it operate safely without supervision during market hours?

If the answer to any is no, you are still building an automated system, not an autonomous agent.

Final Principle

Autonomy is responsibility delegated to code.

The moment you allow a system to decide how capital is deployed without asking you first, you have transferred authority. That authority must be bounded, measurable, and auditable.

An autonomous trading agent is not one that trades alone.

It is one that makes bounded, adaptive decisions in real time while remaining aligned with your objectives and constraints.

1.3 Opportunities and Risks in AI-Based Trading

AI-based trading is attractive for one reason: markets are complex, noisy, and partially observable. Humans struggle with that environment. Machines do not get tired, do not hesitate, and do not panic.

But AI does not remove risk. It changes the shape of it.

This section focuses on where AI provides real, durable advantages—and where it creates new failure modes that are often underestimated.

Opportunities in AI-Based Trading

1. Processing Scale and Complexity

Traditional models struggle with:

- High-dimensional feature spaces
- Nonlinear relationships
- Interactions across assets
- Alternative data streams

AI systems—especially tree-based models and deep learning—handle these better.

Practical examples:

- Combining price, volatility, order flow, macro signals, and sentiment
- Learning nonlinear feature interactions
- Detecting subtle regime changes

Example: combining heterogeneous features

```
import numpy as np

features = np.column_stack([

returns,

volatility,

order_imbalance,

macro_signal,

sentiment_score
```

])

AI models can extract structure from this multi-source input more efficiently than manual rule construction.

Opportunity: broader signal space without manual feature explosion.

2. Adaptive Behavior in Non-Stationary Markets

Markets evolve:

- Volatility regimes shift
- Liquidity conditions change
- Correlations break down

AI models can be retrained or adapted more frequently than traditional statistical systems.

Practical implementation:

- Rolling retraining windows
- Online learning updates
- Regime-switching classifiers

Example: simple rolling retrain pattern

if new_month:

model.fit(recent_data_X, recent_data_y)

This does not guarantee stability, but it allows systematic adaptation instead of fixed-parameter decay.

Opportunity: faster response to structural market changes.

3. Direct Optimization of Trading Objectives

Prediction-based systems optimize accuracy.

AI agents can optimize trading performance directly.

Instead of predicting price direction, an agent can optimize:

- Risk-adjusted return
- Drawdown control
- Inventory balance
- Execution cost

Reward example:

*reward = pnl - 0.5 * volatility - transaction_cost*

This shifts focus from forecasting to decision quality.

Opportunity: alignment between model objective and trading outcome.

4. Automation at Scale

AI allows:

- Multi-asset coverage
- Multi-strategy deployment
- Continuous monitoring
- Automated capital allocation

A single system can manage hundreds of instruments with consistent logic.

Opportunity: operational scalability without proportional staffing increase.

5. Signal Combination and Ensemble Robustness

Markets rarely offer strong standalone signals. Most edges are weak.

AI enables:

- Ensemble models
- Meta-model stacking
- Nonlinear signal blending

Instead of selecting one "best" signal, you combine many weak signals into a stable aggregate.

Opportunity: improved robustness through diversification of signals.

Risks in AI-Based Trading

The opportunities are real. So are the risks—and they are often systemic rather than visible.

1. Overfitting at Scale

AI models are powerful function approximators. That power easily memorizes noise.

Common failure sources:

- Excessive feature engineering
- Small effective sample size
- Unstable market regimes

- Hidden data leakage

Backtests can look exceptional and fail immediately in live trading.

Symptom:

- Performance collapses outside training window
- Sharp degradation after deployment

Mitigation:

- Walk-forward validation
- Strict out-of-sample testing
- Simplicity over complexity
- Feature pruning

AI increases modeling power. It also increases the ability to deceive yourself.

2. Data Leakage and Hidden Bias

AI systems are highly sensitive to subtle biases:

- Look-ahead bias
- Survivorship bias
- Improper timestamp alignment
- Future information in features

Example mistake:

- Using end-of-day volatility to make intraday decisions.

AI models exploit leakage aggressively because they optimize performance metrics blindly.

Mitigation:

- Strict time alignment
- Event-based backtesting
- Audit of feature construction pipeline

If your data is flawed, AI will amplify the flaw.

3. Model Instability and Regime Shift

AI models assume that patterns learned from history persist.

Markets do not guarantee that.

Risk examples:

- Correlation structures break
- Volatility regimes shift
- Policy changes alter liquidity dynamics

Model degradation is often gradual and difficult to detect.

Mitigation:

- Continuous monitoring
- Performance attribution
- Regime detection overlays
- Hard risk constraints

AI increases adaptability, but it does not eliminate structural breaks.

4. Complexity Risk

As systems grow:

- Debugging becomes difficult
- Attribution becomes opaque
- Failures cascade across components

A deep reinforcement learning agent interacting with an execution engine and portfolio allocator introduces multi-layer dependency risk.

Complex systems fail in complex ways.

Mitigation:

- Modular design
- Clear logging
- Isolated testing environments
- Transparent decision traces

If you cannot explain why your system traded, you cannot control it.

5. Operational and Infrastructure Risk

AI trading systems rely on:

- Data feeds
- APIs
- Brokers
- Servers
- Network stability

Autonomous systems magnify infrastructure weaknesses.

Examples:

- Data feed delay leads to poor execution
- API outage causes partial fills
- Latency spike triggers slippage surge

Mitigation:

- Redundant data sources
- Kill switches
- Health monitoring systems
- Graceful degradation logic

AI does not reduce operational risk. It increases exposure to it.

6. Reward Misalignment

If you optimize the wrong objective, the agent will exploit it.

Common mistakes:

- Ignoring transaction costs
- Ignoring tail risk
- Ignoring liquidity constraints
- Rewarding short-term PnL at long-term stability cost

AI agents behave rationally relative to the reward function—not relative to your intention.

Misalignment risk is structural, not technical.

The Trade-Off

AI-based trading offers:

- Higher modeling capacity
- Better scalability
- Direct decision optimization
- Faster adaptation

But it introduces:

- Overfitting risk
- Hidden data bias
- Model decay
- Operational fragility
- Increased system complexity

The net benefit depends entirely on engineering discipline.

Practical Guidance

If you are building AI trading systems:

- Start with execution automation before predictive modeling.
- Introduce ML gradually and measure incremental benefit.
- Enforce hard risk constraints outside the learning loop.
- Monitor degradation continuously.
- Keep systems interpretable enough to debug under stress.

AI is not an edge by itself.

It is a force multiplier—of both good design and bad design.

In trading, that amplification effect is what makes AI powerful—and dangerous.

Chapter 2: Financial Markets and Trading Fundamentals

Before building anything intelligent, I learned the hard way that markets punish ignorance instantly and without apology. I once had a strategy that looked perfect—until execution costs quietly ate all the profits while I celebrated early. Markets don't care about your model. They care about structure, liquidity, and rules.

This chapter covers the core mechanics of financial markets, including instruments, participants, order types, and market microstructure. Understanding these fundamentals is essential for designing agents that operate effectively in real-world conditions.

2.1 Market Structure, Instruments, and Participants

Before you build an agent, you need to understand the environment it operates in. Markets are not abstract price generators. They are structured systems with rules, constraints, incentives, and competing participants.

Most trading failures are not model failures. They are misunderstandings of structure.

This section focuses on three practical foundations:

- How markets are structured
- What instruments agents trade
- Who the other participants are

If your agent ignores any of these, it will trade against forces it does not understand.

1. Market Structure: How Orders Become Prices

At the most basic level, modern financial markets are electronic limit order books.

A limit order book contains:

- Bids (buy orders)
- Asks (sell orders)
- Quantities at each price level

The best bid and best ask define the spread.

Your agent never trades "the market." It trades against resting liquidity provided by other participants.

Core Market Types

Continuous Order-Driven Markets

Most equities and futures markets operate as continuous double auctions.

Orders:

- Match based on price-time priority
- Execute immediately if crossing
- Rest in the book otherwise

Example venues:

- NYSE, NASDAQ, CME

Key implications:

- Liquidity is dynamic
- Spread fluctuates
- Slippage depends on depth

Dealer or Quote-Driven Markets

Common in FX and some fixed income markets.

Market makers provide quotes.

You trade against their inventory.

Implications:

- Spread is often tighter
- Liquidity depends on counterparty
- Execution may be internalized

Your execution logic must adapt depending on venue type.

2. Instruments: What Your Agent Actually Trades

Different instruments behave differently. Design decisions depend heavily on instrument choice.

Equities

Characteristics:

- Centralized exchanges
- Visible order books
- Corporate event risk (earnings, splits)
- Short-selling constraints

Agent considerations:

- Liquidity varies widely by stock
- Borrow availability matters for short positions
- Corporate actions affect backtesting

Futures

Characteristics:

- Standardized contracts
- Leverage embedded
- Expiration dates
- High liquidity in major contracts

Agent considerations:

- Roll logic required
- Margin requirements affect capital allocation
- Contract specifications (tick size, multiplier) affect PnL calculation

Example PnL for a futures position:

*pnl = (exit_price - entry_price) * contract_multiplier * position_size*

Ignoring contract multipliers leads to incorrect risk estimation.

Foreign Exchange (FX)

Characteristics:

- Decentralized market
- 24-hour trading
- Dealer-driven liquidity
- Tight spreads in major pairs

Agent considerations:

- Execution venue affects fill quality
- Spread cost is constant friction
- Macro sensitivity is high

Options

Characteristics:

- Nonlinear payoff

- Time decay
- Volatility exposure
- Multiple strikes and maturities

Agent considerations:

- Greeks (delta, gamma, theta) matter
- Liquidity varies across strikes
- Pricing models influence implied volatility

Options require deeper structural modeling. Avoid them early unless necessary.

3. Market Participants: Who You Compete Against

Your agent is not alone. It competes against other entities with different objectives.

Understanding incentives helps anticipate behavior.

Retail Traders

Characteristics:

- Smaller size
- Often reactive
- Emotion-driven

Impact:

- Can create short-term volatility
- Often concentrated in popular assets

Retail flow may influence short-term momentum but rarely controls long-term pricing.

Institutional Investors

Includes:

- Asset managers
- Pension funds
- Mutual funds

Characteristics:

- Large orders
- Gradual execution
- Benchmark-driven

Impact:

- Create predictable execution patterns
- Generate persistent order flow

Agents can sometimes detect institutional flow via volume patterns or order book imbalance.

Market Makers

Role:

- Provide liquidity
- Capture spread
- Manage inventory risk

Behavior:

- Adjust quotes dynamically
- Hedge exposure rapidly

Your agent trades directly against market makers in many cases.

Understanding spread dynamics is critical for profitability.

High-Frequency Traders (HFTs)

Characteristics:

- Ultra-low latency
- Order book sensitive
- Arbitrage-focused

Impact:

- Reduce spreads
- Compete on microsecond horizons

If your agent operates at low frequency (minutes to hours), competing directly with HFTs is unnecessary. But at sub-second horizons, you are competing in their domain.

Other AI Systems

You are not the only one using machine learning.

Modern markets contain:

- Statistical arbitrage funds
- Execution algorithms
- Reinforcement learning agents
- Adaptive market makers

This creates reflexivity:

- Models influence markets, which influence models.

Edges decay faster when widely adopted.

4. Practical Implications for Agent Design

Liquidity Awareness

Never design an agent without incorporating liquidity.

Key metrics:

- Average daily volume
- Order book depth
- Spread
- Slippage estimates

Example liquidity constraint:

*max_position = 0.01 * average_daily_volume*

Position sizing must respect market capacity.

Transaction Cost Awareness

Costs include:

- Spread
- Commission
- Slippage
- Market impact

Ignoring these converts profitable signals into losing trades.

Always subtract estimated costs before labeling a strategy profitable.

Trading Hours and Session Structure

Markets open and close.

Liquidity changes throughout the day.

Intraday patterns matter:

- **Open:** volatile
- **Midday:** lower volume
- **Close:** increased activity

Agents should account for session timing.

Regulatory and Structural Constraints

Depending on instrument and jurisdiction:

- Short-selling restrictions
- Circuit breakers
- Position limits
- Margin requirements

Autonomous systems must encode these rules explicitly.

5. Minimum Structural Checklist Before Building Models

Before writing a single ML model, confirm:

- You understand how orders are matched.
- You know the liquidity profile of your instrument.
- You can calculate true transaction cost.
- You know who your primary counterparties are.
- You have encoded structural constraints into your system.

If any of these are unclear, do not move to modeling yet.

Final Principle

Markets are competitive ecosystems.

Prices are not abstract signals to predict.

They are outcomes of interacting participants under specific structural rules.

An AI trading agent that ignores market structure is like a self-driving car that ignores traffic laws.

You are not modeling prices.

You are modeling behavior within a structured, adversarial system.

Everything in the next chapters builds on that reality.

2.2 Order Types, Liquidity, and Market Microstructure

Most strategy ideas look good before execution. They break the moment they meet the order book.

If you don't understand how orders interact with liquidity at the micro level, your agent will consistently pay more than expected, get partially filled, or move the market against itself.

This section focuses on three practical layers:

- Order types and how they behave
- Liquidity and its hidden costs
- Microstructure mechanics that directly affect profitability

1. Order Types: How You Enter the Market

Your agent does not trade "at the current price." It submits an order that interacts with the book.

Market Orders

A market order executes immediately against the best available liquidity.

Pros:

- Guaranteed execution (if liquidity exists)
- Simple logic
- Useful in fast-moving markets

Cons:

- Pays the spread
- Subject to slippage
- Can walk the book if size is large

Example slippage:

execution_price = best_ask + impact_adjustment

Market orders are speed-focused, not cost-focused.

Use when:

- Urgency matters

- Size is small relative to liquidity
- Exiting risk is priority

Limit Orders

A limit order specifies the maximum buy price or minimum sell price.

Pros:

- Controls price
- May capture spread
- Lower transaction cost

Cons:

- No execution guarantee
- Risk of non-fill
- Adverse selection risk

Example:

limit_price = best_bid

You post at the bid and wait.

Key trade-off:

- Fill probability vs price improvement.

Stop Orders

Triggered when price crosses a threshold.

Used for:

- Risk control
- Breakout strategies

Risk:

- In fast markets, stop orders can execute at worse-than-expected prices due to gaps.

Iceberg Orders

Large orders broken into smaller visible pieces.

Used to:

- Reduce market impact
- Hide true size

Requires broker or exchange support.

Immediate-Or-Cancel (IOC) and Fill-Or-Kill (FOK)

IOC:

- Execute available quantity immediately; cancel remainder.

FOK:

- Execute entire order immediately or cancel completely.

Useful for:

Liquidity-sensitive strategies

Avoiding partial fills

2. Liquidity: What It Really Means

Liquidity is not just volume. It is:

- Depth at each price level
- Spread stability
- Fill probability
- Market resilience after trades

Spread

Spread = Best Ask – Best Bid

Every market order pays the spread.

Example:

- **If bid** = 100.00
- **Ask** = 100.02

Spread cost per share = 0.02

For 10,000 shares:

- Cost = 200 before fees.

Agents must account for spread before deciding trade frequency.

Depth

Order book depth determines how much size you can execute without moving price.

If best ask has only 500 shares and you buy 5,000:

- You will climb multiple price levels.

Impact example:

*avg_execution_price = sum(price_i * qty_i) / total_qty*

Large orders create worse average prices.

Market Impact

Impact occurs when your own trade moves price.

Two types:

- Temporary impact
- Permanent impact

Temporary impact:

- Price reverts after liquidity replenishes.

Permanent impact:

- Your trade signals information to the market.

Impact grows nonlinearly with size.

Rule of thumb:

- Do not trade more than a small fraction of average daily volume.

Example constraint:

*max_trade_size = 0.02 * average_daily_volume*

3. Market Microstructure: The Hidden Layer

Microstructure studies how trading rules and order flow shape price formation.

Your agent competes at this level whether you model it or not.

Price-Time Priority

Most exchanges match orders based on:

- Best price
- Earliest timestamp

If you post a limit order at the bid but are late in queue, you may not get filled.

Queue position matters.

Agents posting liquidity must account for fill probability.

Order Flow Imbalance

Short-term price movement often correlates with imbalance between aggressive buyers and sellers.

Simple imbalance metric:

imbalance = (bid_volume - ask_volume) / (bid_volume + ask_volume)

Positive imbalance may signal upward pressure.

Microstructure-aware agents include this in state representation.

Adverse Selection

If your limit order gets filled, ask why.

Often it fills because:

- Someone with better information aggressively trades against you.

Example:

- You post buy limit at 100.
- Price quickly drops to 99.80.
- You were filled right before decline.

Your fill was not random.

Liquidity provision earns spread but exposes you to informed flow.

Latency

Latency determines how quickly your order reaches the exchange.

In high-frequency contexts:

- Microseconds matter.

In medium-frequency strategies:

- Infrastructure stability matters more than speed.

Never design a microsecond strategy on retail infrastructure.

Hidden Liquidity

- Some liquidity is not visible in the public order book.
- Dark pools and internalizers match orders off-exchange.
- Execution quality may vary significantly by venue.
- Agents that scale must monitor venue-level performance.

4. Practical Execution Trade-Offs

Every order choice balances:

- Execution certainty
- Cost
- Speed
- Information leakage

Market order:

- High certainty, higher cost.

Limit order:

- Lower cost, lower certainty.

Large order:

- Higher impact.

Small order:

- Higher time risk.

Your agent must explicitly encode these trade-offs.

5. Microstructure-Aware Agent Design

Before deploying a strategy, confirm:

- Expected edge per trade exceeds spread + fees.

- Trade size fits inside typical depth.
- Slippage assumptions match historical execution.
- Fill probability is realistically modeled.
- Order type is aligned with strategy horizon.

Short-term strategies are more sensitive to microstructure than long-term ones.

Final Principle

At the modeling stage, everything looks clean.

At the execution stage, every trade interacts with:

- Spread
- Queue priority
- Competing order flow
- Liquidity depth
- Market impact

Profitability is not determined only by signal quality.

It is determined by how that signal survives contact with the order book.

If your agent does not understand microstructure, the market will teach it—expensively.

2.3 Trading Styles: Discretionary, Systematic, and Agent-Based

Before building AI trading agents, you need clarity on one fundamental question:

What kind of decision-maker are you replacing—or augmenting?

Trading styles evolve along a spectrum:

- Discretionary
- Systematic
- Agent-based

Each style represents a different philosophy of decision-making, control, and adaptation. Understanding the differences prevents you from mixing incompatible assumptions in your system design.

1. Discretionary Trading

Discretionary trading is human-driven decision-making.

A discretionary trader:

- Interprets charts, news, macro events
- Adjusts position sizes subjectively
- Overrides plans when "conditions feel different"
- Reacts to intuition

Strengths

- Flexible interpretation of complex events
- Ability to adapt instantly to new information
- Incorporates qualitative insights

Humans are good at contextual reasoning and handling ambiguity.

Weaknesses

- Emotional bias
- Inconsistent execution
- Poor scalability

- Hard to backtest

Two discretionary traders can see the same chart and take opposite actions.

From an engineering perspective, discretionary trading is:

- Not reproducible
- Not auditable
- Not scalable

AI systems are often built to remove these weaknesses.

2. Systematic Trading

Systematic trading replaces intuition with explicit rules.

Decisions are:

- Defined by formulas
- Backtestable
- Reproducible
- Consistent

Example rule-based strategy:

if short_ma > long_ma:

position = 1

else:

position = 0

Every input produces a deterministic output.

Strengths

- Repeatability
- Statistical validation
- Controlled risk management
- Easy to monitor

Systematic strategies remove emotional variance.

Weaknesses

- Static assumptions
- Parameter fragility
- Limited adaptability
- Hard-coded logic

Most systematic systems rely on fixed parameters. When market regimes shift, performance degrades until the system is manually adjusted.

Systematic trading improved discipline. It did not solve adaptability.

3. Agent-Based Trading

Agent-based trading introduces autonomy and feedback-driven adaptation.

An agent:

- Observes structured state
- Chooses actions
- Receives reward feedback
- Adjusts behavior

It does not just follow rules. It optimizes behavior within constraints.

Core loop:

state = observe()

action = policy(state)

reward = compute_reward()

update_policy(state, action, reward)

This creates a closed feedback system.

Key Differences in Decision Logic

Discretionary

- **Decision source**: Human interpretation
- **Adaptation:** Immediate but subjective
- **Execution:** Manual or semi-automated

Systematic

- **Decision source:** Fixed logic
- **Adaptation:** Manual parameter updates
- **Execution:** Automated

Agent-Based

- **Decision source**: Learned or adaptive policy
- **Adaptation**: Continuous or scheduled
- **Execution**: Fully automated

Adaptability Comparison

Discretionary traders adapt quickly—but inconsistently.

Systematic traders adapt slowly—through redesign and re-optimization.

Agent-based systems adapt mechanically—through data-driven updates.

However, adaptation introduces risk:

- Poor reward design
- Instability during regime shifts
- Drift without supervision

Autonomy requires constraints.

Practical Design Implications

When Discretionary Logic Makes Sense

- Low-frequency macro strategies
- Event-driven trading
- Illiquid assets requiring negotiation

Fully automating subjective macro reasoning is difficult.

Even AI systems often use human oversight at this level.

When Systematic Trading Is Sufficient

- Medium-frequency equity strategies
- Statistically stable signals
- Execution algorithms

- Risk overlays

Many profitable systems remain systematic with minor ML enhancements.

Complexity is not mandatory for profitability.

When Agent-Based Systems Add Value

Agent-based systems are most useful when:

- State space is large
- Relationships are nonlinear
- Environment changes frequently
- Action optimization matters more than prediction

Examples:

- Intraday market-making
- Adaptive position sizing
- Multi-asset allocation
- Reinforcement learning execution

If the environment is stable and well understood, a systematic model may outperform a complex agent simply because it is easier to control.

Hybrid Systems: The Real-World Standard

In practice, production systems are hybrids.

Example architecture:

- Systematic signal generation
- Agent-based position sizing
- Hard-coded risk constraints
- Execution algorithm optimized separately

This layered approach avoids full autonomy while capturing adaptability where needed.

Control vs Flexibility Trade-Off

The more autonomy you introduce, the more:

- Monitoring you need

- Logging you require
- Constraints you must enforce

Agent-based systems increase flexibility. They also increase uncertainty.

A practical framework:

- Use rules for risk control.
- Use ML for signal extraction.
- Use agents for decision optimization where feedback is reliable.

Common Mistakes When Transitioning to Agents

- Replacing stable rule-based systems unnecessarily.
- Introducing learning without proper monitoring.
- Allowing agents to control risk constraints.
- Optimizing short-term reward at the cost of stability.
- Not every systematic strategy should become an agent.

Autonomy is useful when the environment demands it—not because the technology exists.

Decision-Making Maturity Model

You can think of progression as:

- Human judgment → Deterministic rules → Statistical models → Adaptive agents

Each step increases:

- Scalability
- Automation
- Engineering complexity
- Monitoring requirements

There is no universal best style. The correct approach depends on:

- Strategy horizon
- Asset class
- Liquidity

- Infrastructure capability
- Risk tolerance
- Final Principle
- Discretionary trading relies on human cognition.
- Systematic trading relies on explicit logic.
- Agent-based trading relies on adaptive decision systems.

The goal of this book is not to eliminate systematic thinking. It is to extend it.

Agent-based systems are systematic trading systems with feedback-driven autonomy layered on top.

Used correctly, they combine discipline with adaptability.

Used carelessly, they amplify mistakes faster than any human ever could.

Chapter 3: Data Sources for AI Trading Systems

At some point, I realized most trading problems aren't model problems—they're data problems wearing disguises. Bad timestamps, missing values, survivorship bias, and "helpful" datasets that accidentally leak the future. Data has a way of sabotaging you while pretending to help.

This chapter explores market and alternative data sources, discusses common data pitfalls, and explains how data quality, latency, and bias directly affect agent performance.

3.1 Market Data: Price, Volume, and Order Book

Most trading models fail before training begins. Not because the algorithm is weak, but because the data is misunderstood.

Market data is not just "price history." It is a layered representation of transactions, intent, and liquidity. If your agent consumes poorly structured data, it will learn distorted patterns.

This section focuses on the three core data categories every AI trading system must handle correctly:

- Price data
- Volume data
- Order book data

Each has different structure, noise characteristics, and use cases.

1. Price Data

Price is the most accessible and most misunderstood market variable.

Types of Price Data

Trade Price (Last Price)

The price of the most recent executed trade.

Common mistake:

- Treating last price as a stable representation of market value. In thin markets, a single small trade can distort it.

Bid and Ask Prices

Best available buy (bid) and sell (ask) quotes.

More informative than last price because they reflect current supply and demand.

Mid-price calculation:

mid_price = (best_bid + best_ask) / 2

Mid-price is often preferred in modeling to reduce spread noise.

OHLC Data (Candlestick Data)

Open, High, Low, Close for a fixed time interval.

Useful for:

- Low-frequency strategies
- Historical backtesting
- Feature engineering

Limitation:

OHLC compresses intraperiod behavior. It hides order flow and path dependency.

Two candles with identical OHLC values can have very different intrabar dynamics.

Time-Based vs Event-Based Sampling

Most datasets are time-based (e.g., 1-minute bars). But markets do not move in fixed time intervals. They move when trades occur.

Alternative sampling methods:

- **Tick-based** (every trade)
- **Volume-based** (after X shares traded)
- **Dollar-based** (after X dollars traded)

Volume bars often reduce heteroskedasticity compared to fixed time bars.

Returns Instead of Raw Prices

Most models operate on returns rather than prices.

Log return example:

```
import numpy as np

log_return = np.log(price_t / price_t_minus_1)
```

Returns:

- Improve stationarity
- Normalize scale differences
- Reduce trend bias

Always verify alignment when calculating returns to avoid look-ahead errors.

2. Volume Data

Volume measures how much was traded, not how price moved.

It is a proxy for participation and conviction.

Why Volume Matters

- Price movement without volume is fragile.
- Price movement with strong volume suggests broader participation.

Common derived metrics:

- Volume moving average
- Volume spikes
- Relative volume (current vs historical average)

Example relative volume:

relative_volume = current_volume / avg_volume_20

High relative volume may signal:

- Breakouts
- News-driven activity
- Institutional participation
- Volume and Liquidity

Volume helps estimate liquidity, but it is not the full picture.

High volume does not guarantee:

- Tight spreads
- Deep order books
- Low impact

Liquidity must be measured alongside spread and depth.

Volume-Based Features

Practical features include:

- Volume-weighted average price (VWAP)
- Volume imbalance
- Volume acceleration

VWAP example:

*vwap = (price * volume).sum() / volume.sum()*

VWAP is widely used in execution benchmarking.

Agents should track deviation from VWAP for intraday positioning.

3. Order Book Data

Order book data reveals supply and demand before trades occur.

It contains:

- **Bid levels** (price and quantity)
- **Ask levels** (price and quantity)

Example simplified structure:

order_book = {

"bids": [(100.00, 500), (99.99, 1000)],

"asks": [(100.02, 400), (100.03, 900)]

}

Level 1 vs Level 2 Data

Level 1:

- Best bid
- Best ask
- Last trade

Level 2:

- Multiple price levels
- Full depth information

For microstructure-aware strategies, Level 2 data is essential.

Order Book Imbalance

A common microstructure feature:

imbalance = (bid_volume - ask_volume) / (bid_volume + ask_volume)

Positive imbalance may indicate short-term upward pressure.

Imbalance works best for short-horizon strategies.

Spread Dynamics

Spread width fluctuates with:

- Volatility
- Liquidity
- Time of day

Spread is not constant friction. It is state-dependent.

Agents must track spread regime to adjust position size or trade frequency.

Order Flow vs Order Book

Important distinction:

- Order book shows intent.
- Order flow shows executed aggression.

Aggressive trades that consume liquidity often drive short-term price movement more than passive quotes.

If possible, track:

- Market buy volume
- Market sell volume
- Trade aggressor side

This provides insight into directional pressure.

4. Data Quality Challenges

Market data is messy.

Common problems:

- Missing ticks
- Out-of-order timestamps
- Duplicate entries
- Corporate action adjustments
- Survivorship bias

Before modeling, verify:

- Timestamp alignment
- Correct timezone normalization
- Proper handling of splits and dividends
- No forward-looking contamination

Example cleaning step:

data = data.sort_values("timestamp").drop_duplicates()

Data validation is not optional. It is structural risk management.

5. Matching Data to Strategy Horizon

Different strategies require different data granularity.

Low-frequency strategies:

- Daily OHLC
- Adjusted close prices
- Volume averages

Intraday strategies:

- Minute bars
- VWAP tracking
- Spread monitoring

High-frequency strategies:

- Tick data
- Level 2 order book
- Trade aggressor flags

Over-collecting high-resolution data increases noise and infrastructure cost without guaranteed edge.

Match data resolution to decision frequency.

6. Practical Data Pipeline Checklist

Before training any model:

- Define sampling method (time, tick, volume).
- Confirm no look-ahead bias.

- Adjust for corporate actions.
- Validate spread and transaction cost assumptions.
- Verify liquidity supports intended position sizes.

Data defines what your agent can learn. If the data lacks relevant structure, no model will recover it.

Final Principle

- Price shows what happened.
- Volume shows how much conviction existed.
- Order book shows what may happen next.

A robust AI trading system does not treat these as interchangeable.

It understands the information hierarchy and aligns data selection with strategy objectives.

Everything else—features, models, agents—depends on getting this layer correct first.

3.2 Alternative Data: News, Sentiment, and Macroeconomic Signals

If price and volume tell you what happened, alternative data tries to explain why it happened—or what might happen next.

Alternative data can provide incremental edge, but it also introduces new risks: noise, latency, overfitting, and spurious correlations. Used carelessly, it adds complexity without improving performance.

This section focuses on three major categories:

- News data
- Sentiment data
- Macroeconomic signals

The goal is practical integration, not theoretical novelty.

1. News Data

Markets react to information shocks. News is often the source.

Examples:

- Earnings announcements
- M&A events
- Regulatory changes
- Geopolitical developments

Structured vs Unstructured News

Structured news:

- Earnings beats/misses
- Economic calendar releases
- Dividend announcements

Unstructured news:

- Headlines
- Full articles
- Press releases

Structured news is easier to model. Unstructured news requires NLP processing.

Basic News Processing Pipeline

A simple NLP workflow:

- Collect timestamped headlines
- Clean text
- Convert to numerical representation
- Generate sentiment or topic score

Example using a simplified sentiment score:

sentiment_score = sentiment_model.predict(headline_text)

You must ensure:

- Timestamp accuracy (when was it published?)
- Market availability (was it public before the trade decision?)

Many datasets introduce subtle look-ahead bias.

Event-Based Modeling

Instead of continuous prediction, treat news as discrete events.

Example approach:

if earnings_surprise > threshold:

signal = 1

else:

signal = 0

Event-based trading reduces noise compared to continuous headline monitoring.

Practical Limitations of News

- Reaction is often priced in within seconds.
- Latency matters significantly.
- Retail-grade infrastructure struggles to compete on breaking news.

For most medium-frequency strategies, news is more useful for regime filtering than microsecond reaction.

2. Sentiment Data

Sentiment attempts to quantify crowd psychology.

Sources:

- Social media
- Financial forums
- News tone
- Analyst reports

Sentiment can capture:

- Retail enthusiasm
- Panic
- Narrative shifts
- Sentiment Score Construction

Basic workflow:

- Collect text corpus
- Tokenize and preprocess
- Use model to assign polarity score
- Aggregate over time window

Example aggregation:

daily_sentiment = sentiment_scores.mean()

Aggregation is critical. Individual messages are noisy. Signal emerges from distribution shifts.

Lag and Decay

Sentiment effects are often short-lived.

Agents should apply decay functions:

*adjusted_sentiment = raw_sentiment * np.exp(-decay_rate * time_since_signal)*

Without decay, stale sentiment contaminates the model.

Risk of Spurious Correlation

Social sentiment spikes often occur after price moves.

If you do not align timestamps precisely, you may end up modeling reaction rather than prediction.

Always test:

- Does sentiment lead price?
- Or does it follow price?

Causality direction matters.

3. Macroeconomic Signals

Macroeconomic data influences:

- Interest rates
- Inflation expectations
- Currency valuation
- Equity risk premiums

Examples:

- CPI releases
- GDP reports
- Employment data
- Central bank decisions

Scheduled Economic Releases

Economic calendar events are predictable in timing.

This allows pre-event and post-event modeling.

Example:

if time_to_event < 30_minutes:

reduce_position_size()

Macroeconomic events increase volatility and spread. Even if not traded directly, agents should adapt risk during these windows.

Surprise Modeling

Markets respond to deviation from expectations, not absolute values.

Economic surprise example:

surprise = actual_value - consensus_estimate

Magnitude and direction of surprise often drive short-term price reactions.

Regime-Level Influence

Macro signals are better suited for:

- Regime classification
- Asset allocation shifts
- Risk-on / risk-off filtering

Example:

if inflation_trend > threshold:

*equity_exposure *= 0.7*

Macro signals usually operate on slower timescales than intraday strategies.

4. Integration Into Trading Systems

Alternative data should not replace price-based signals blindly.

Better integration patterns:

- Use macro data for regime filtering.
- Use sentiment as secondary confirmation.
- Use news for event-driven triggers.
- Combine weak signals through weighted ensemble.

Example weighted combination:

combined_signal = (

*0.5 * price_signal +*

*0.3 * sentiment_signal +*

*0.2 * macro_signal*

)

Weights should be validated out-of-sample.

5. Infrastructure Considerations

Alternative data introduces additional requirements:

- Storage for text data

- NLP processing capability
- Timestamp synchronization
- Event alignment mechanisms

Before adding alternative data, confirm:

- It improves out-of-sample performance.
- The signal survives transaction costs.
- Latency matches strategy horizon.
- Complexity does not exceed incremental benefit.

Many systems become fragile because alternative data increases dimensionality without proportional signal gain.

6. When Alternative Data Adds Real Value

Alternative data is most useful when:

- Trading event-driven strategies
- Running medium-frequency models
- Managing multi-asset portfolios
- Detecting macro regime shifts

It is less useful when:

- Competing in ultra-high-frequency trading
- Running purely statistical mean-reversion models
- Trading highly efficient large-cap equities without latency advantage

Final Principle

Alternative data expands the state space of your agent.

- It can provide informational edge—but only if:
- It is properly aligned in time.
- It leads price rather than reacts to it.
- It is integrated with discipline.
- It survives realistic backtesting.

More data does not automatically mean more alpha.

Alternative data should enhance decision quality—not distract from structural market realities established in the previous chapters.

3.3 Data Quality, Latency, and Survivorship Bias

Most AI trading systems do not fail because of poor modeling. They fail because the data quietly lied. Bad timestamps. Missing records. Survivorship bias. Unrealistic latency assumptions.

These errors rarely trigger visible exceptions. They simply produce inflated backtests and fragile live performance.

If you want your agent to survive outside a notebook, this section matters more than model selection.

We will focus on three structural risks:

- Data quality
- Latency
- Survivorship bias

1. Data Quality: Garbage In, Amplified Out

Machine learning models are extremely sensitive to subtle distortions.

Common Data Quality Issues

- Missing timestamps
- Duplicate records
- Out-of-order trades
- Incorrect timezone alignment
- Corporate actions not adjusted
- Inconsistent symbol mappings

These errors rarely crash your code. They distort learning.

Timestamp Integrity

All financial modeling is time-dependent. Even a one-minute misalignment can introduce hidden look-ahead bias.

Example mistake:

- Using closing price at 16:00
- Generating signal at 15:59
- Backtest assumes signal had access to the close

That is forward leakage.

Always enforce:

data = data.sort_values("timestamp")

data = data.drop_duplicates()

Then verify that:

- Features at time t only use data available at or before t.
- Targets are strictly forward-looking.

Corporate Actions

If you trade equities, you must adjust for:

- Stock splits
- Dividends
- Mergers

Unadjusted price data creates artificial jumps.

Example split adjustment logic:

adjusted_price = raw_price / split_factor

If your historical prices are not adjusted consistently, your model will learn patterns that do not exist in live trading.

Missing Data and Forward Fill Risk

Forward filling missing values can introduce bias.

Example:

data.fillna(method="ffill")

This may incorrectly assume that stale information remains valid.

Better approach:

- Identify why data is missing.
- Treat structural missingness differently from random gaps.
- Consider dropping affected samples instead of filling blindly.

2. Latency: The Hidden Assumption in Every Backtest

Backtests assume immediate execution. Real markets do not.

Latency includes:

- Data feed delay
- Signal computation time
- Order routing time
- Exchange processing time

If your backtest assumes zero latency, it is optimistic.

Modeling Execution Delay

Instead of executing at the same bar as the signal:

execution_price = price.shift(-1)

This assumes execution at next period open.

For intraday systems, simulate delay explicitly.

Example:

execution_time = signal_time + latency_delta

execution_price = price_at(execution_time)

Without modeling latency, short-horizon strategies appear more profitable than they are.

Spread and Slippage Interaction

Latency increases:

- Slippage
- Adverse selection
- Missed fills

If your strategy depends on tight spreads and quick reaction, infrastructure matters.

Retail-grade infrastructure cannot support microsecond-sensitive strategies.

Match latency assumptions to reality.

Data Timestamp vs Receipt Timestamp

Important distinction:

- **Exchange timestamp** = when event occurred.
- **Receipt timestamp** = when your system received it.

If you backtest on exchange timestamps but trade on delayed feeds, your historical simulation is misaligned.

3. Survivorship Bias: The Silent Performance Inflator

Survivorship bias occurs when you only analyze assets that still exist today.

Example:

- If you backtest using the current S&P 500 constituents over the past 15 years, you exclude:
- Bankrupt companies
- Delisted stocks
- Merged entities

This artificially improves historical returns.

Why It Matters

Companies that disappear usually underperform before they disappear.

Removing them inflates:

- Average returns
- Strategy stability
- Signal effectiveness

Correct Approach

- Use historical index membership.

At time t:

- Only include assets that existed at time t.
- Include delisted assets in your historical universe.

Your dataset must reflect the real investable universe at each historical point.

4. Look-Ahead Bias: A Close Relative

Look-ahead bias occurs when future information leaks into features.

Common examples:

- Using final earnings numbers before release date.
- Using revised macro data instead of original releases.

- Calculating rolling statistics using future observations.

Example mistake:

rolling_mean = price.rolling(window=20).mean()

signal = price > rolling_mean

If not shifted correctly, the rolling mean includes the current observation, contaminating the signal.

Corrected version:

rolling_mean = price.rolling(window=20).mean().shift(1)

Every feature must respect chronological order.

5. Data Revision Bias

Macroeconomic data is often revised after initial release.

Backtests using final revised values assume perfect hindsight.

If trading economic releases, use:

- Real-time historical release data
- First-reported values, not revised values

Otherwise, your macro strategy is unknowingly cheating.

6. Practical Validation Checklist

Before training any model, confirm:

- Data is chronologically sorted.
- No duplicates or timestamp overlaps exist.
- All features are shifted appropriately.
- Corporate actions are adjusted correctly.
- Universe selection reflects historical reality.
- Execution delay is modeled realistically.
- Transaction costs and spread are included.

If any of these are skipped, backtest performance is suspect.

7. Stress Testing Data Integrity

Introduce controlled perturbations:

- Randomly drop 1% of rows.
- Introduce slight timestamp shifts.
- Increase assumed latency.
- Increase transaction costs.

If performance collapses under minor disturbances, your strategy is fragile.

Robust strategies degrade gradually, not catastrophically.

Final Principle

Models do not fail randomly. They fail because assumptions embedded in data were unrealistic.

Data quality determines:

- What your agent sees
- What it learns
- How it generalizes

Latency determines:

- What price it actually trades

Survivorship bias determines:

- Whether your historical edge was real

Before optimizing models, optimize truthfulness of data.

In trading systems, data integrity is not preprocessing.

It is structural risk management.

Chapter 4: Data Engineering and Feature Construction

This is the chapter where raw chaos slowly becomes something useful. Feature engineering isn't glamorous. It's mostly cleaning, aligning, transforming, and wondering why everything breaks when you add one more feature. Still, this is where agents either gain an edge—or drown in noise.

This chapter focuses on preparing financial data for modeling, constructing meaningful features, and reducing dimensionality while preserving signal relevance.

4.1 Cleaning, Normalizing, and Aligning Time-Series Data

Raw financial data is chaotic. Different frequencies, different timezones, missing values, corporate actions, asynchronous updates.

If you feed that directly into a model, you are not training on markets—you are training on inconsistencies.

This chapter focuses on three operational steps that must happen before modeling:

- Cleaning
- Normalizing
- Time alignment

These are engineering tasks, not academic exercises. They determine whether your system behaves reliably in production.

1. Cleaning Time-Series Data

Cleaning is about structural integrity, not cosmetic fixes.

Step 1: Sort and Deduplicate

Always start by enforcing chronological order.

data = data.sort_values("timestamp")

data = data.drop_duplicates(subset="timestamp")

Out-of-order data introduces false patterns in rolling statistics and model training.

Step 2: Handle Missing Values

Financial data often contains gaps due to:

- Trading halts
- Illiquid periods
- Data feed outages

Do not blindly forward-fill everything.

Bad practice:

data.fillna(method="ffill")

Better approach:

- **For price data**: forward fill cautiously for small gaps.
- **For volume**: missing often means zero, not previous value.
- **For features**: evaluate whether missingness carries information.

Example:

```
data["volume"] = data["volume"].fillna(0)
```

Missing data policy should match economic meaning.

Step 3: Remove Bad Ticks and Outliers

Occasional data errors can create extreme spikes.

Example filter:

```
data = data[(data["price"] > 0)]
data = data[abs(data["return"]) < 0.2]
```

The threshold must be realistic. Removing legitimate high-volatility events is also a mistake.

A more robust method uses rolling statistics:

```
rolling_std = data["return"].rolling(50).std()
data = data[abs(data["return"]) < 5 * rolling_std]
```

Cleaning must remove errors, not real volatility.

Step 4: Adjust for Corporate Actions

For equities:

- Stock splits
- Dividends
- Mergers

Adjusted price series must be consistent across time.

If using adjusted close:

- Ensure open, high, and low are adjusted proportionally.
- Confirm volume is adjusted when required.

Unadjusted splits create artificial return shocks.

2. Normalizing Financial Data

Raw prices are scale-dependent and non-stationary. Most machine learning models perform better with normalized inputs.

Why Normalization Matters

- Different assets trade at different price levels.
- Volatility changes over time.
- Features with large magnitude dominate training.

Normalization stabilizes learning.

Method 1: Returns Instead of Prices

Convert price to returns:

data["log_return"] = np.log(data["price"] / data["price"].shift(1))

Returns reduce trend effects and improve stationarity.

Method 2: Z-Score Normalization

Standardization within a rolling window:

rolling_mean = data["feature"].rolling(100).mean().shift(1)

rolling_std = data["feature"].rolling(100).std().shift(1)

data["feature_z"] = (data["feature"] - rolling_mean) / rolling_std

Important:

- Always shift rolling statistics to prevent look-ahead bias.
- Z-scoring makes features comparable across time.

Method 3: Min-Max Scaling

Used less frequently in finance because price ranges shift.

scaled = (feature - min_value) / (max_value - min_value)

Avoid using global min and max computed over entire dataset. That introduces future information.

If necessary, compute within rolling windows.

Volatility Scaling

Normalize signals relative to current volatility:

vol = data["log_return"].rolling(50).std().shift(1)

data["vol_scaled_return"] = data["log_return"] / vol

THIS HELPS MAINTAIN consistent behavior across volatility regimes.

3. Aligning Multi-Source Time-Series Data

Real trading systems combine:

- Price data
- Volume data
- Macro indicators
- Sentiment signals
- Alternative data

These do not update at the same frequency.

Alignment is where many subtle biases enter.

Timezone Consistency

All timestamps must be converted to a common timezone.

data["timestamp"] = data["timestamp"].dt.tz_convert("UTC")

Mixing local exchange time with UTC leads to silent errors.

Resampling to Common Frequency

Example: Convert tick data to 5-minute bars.

bars = data.resample("5T", on="timestamp").agg({

"price": "last",

"volume": "sum"

})

Resampling must preserve economic meaning.

- **Price** → last
- **Volume** → sum
- **High** → max
- **Low** → min

Incorrect aggregation creates distorted features.

Forward Alignment of Signals

Macro data released monthly must not influence earlier timestamps.

Incorrect merge:

merged = price_data.merge(macro_data, on="date", how="left")

Correct approach:

- Forward-fill only after release timestamp.

macro_data = macro_data.set_index("release_time")

merged = price_data.join(macro_data, how="left")

merged = merged.ffill()

But ensure forward fill only occurs after release time.

Release-aware alignment is critical.

Multi-Asset Alignment

When building cross-sectional models:

- Ensure all assets are aligned to the same timestamp grid.
- Handle assets that do not trade during certain intervals.

Example:

panel = panel.groupby("asset").apply(lambda x: x.resample("1D").last())

Missing days for illiquid assets must be handled explicitly.

4. Data Leakage Prevention During Alignment

Most leakage happens during feature construction.

Rules:

- Any rolling statistic must be shifted.
- Any merge must respect release time.
- Any future-dependent transformation must be avoided.

Example safe pattern:

data["rolling_mean"] = data["price"].rolling(20).mean().shift(1)

If you forget .shift(1), your model is cheating.

5. Production Consistency

Cleaning and normalization steps must be:

- Deterministic
- Reproducible
- Identical in backtest and live trading

Mismatch between training pipeline and production pipeline causes performance drift.

Best practice:

Encapsulate preprocessing in reusable functions:

def preprocess(data):

 # cleaning

 # normalization

 # alignment

return processed_data

Use the same function in both training and live execution.

6. Practical Pre-Model Checklist

Before training:

- Data is chronologically sorted.
- Missing values are handled intentionally.
- Corporate actions are adjusted.
- Features are normalized without leakage.
- Multi-source data is aligned correctly.
- All rolling metrics are shifted.
- Preprocessing is identical in live environment.

If preprocessing is inconsistent, no model architecture will fix it.

Final Principle

- Cleaning ensures correctness.

- Normalization ensures stability.
- Alignment ensures honesty.
- Feature engineering builds signals.
- But preprocessing builds trust in those signals.

In AI trading systems, data preparation is not a support task.

It is the foundation on which every downstream decision depends.

4.2 Feature Engineering for Market Prediction

Models do not discover alpha from raw price series. They learn from structured representations of behavior. Feature engineering is the process of converting raw market data into informative signals.

This is where most practical edge is created—or destroyed.

Feature engineering in trading should focus on three principles:

- Economic meaning
- Stability across regimes
- Real-time computability

If a feature has no economic interpretation, is unstable, or cannot be computed live without leakage, it does not belong in your model.

1. Return-Based Features

The most fundamental input to any market model is return.

Simple and Log Returns

data["return_1"] = data["price"].pct_change()

data["log_return_1"] = np.log(data["price"] / data["price"].shift(1))

Multiple horizons:

data["return_5"] = data["price"].pct_change(5)

data["return_20"] = data["price"].pct_change(20)

Multi-horizon returns capture momentum and mean-reversion effects across timescales.

Always shift features if used for prediction:

data["return_5"] = data["price"].pct_change(5).shift(1)

2. Momentum Features

Momentum is one of the most persistent empirical effects in financial markets.

Basic momentum:

data["momentum_20"] = data["price"] / data["price"].shift(20) - 1

Smoothed momentum using moving averages:

```
short_ma = data["price"].rolling(10).mean().shift(1)
long_ma = data["price"].rolling(50).mean().shift(1)
data["ma_ratio"] = short_ma / long_ma - 1
```

Interpretation:

- Positive values suggest upward trend.
- Negative values suggest downward trend.

Momentum features work best in trending regimes. In choppy markets, they generate false signals.

3. Volatility Features

Volatility affects risk, position sizing, and signal reliability.

Rolling realized volatility:

```
data["volatility_20"] = data["log_return_1"].rolling(20).std().shift(1)
```

Volatility regime feature:

```
long_vol = data["log_return_1"].rolling(100).std().shift(1)
data["vol_regime"] = data["volatility_20"] / long_vol
```

High volatility regimes often require smaller position sizes.

Volatility can also serve as a filter: avoid strategies when volatility exceeds threshold.

4. Volume and Liquidity Features

Volume provides context to price movement.

Relative volume:

```
avg_vol = data["volume"].rolling(20).mean().shift(1)
data["rel_volume"] = data["volume"] / avg_vol
```

Price-volume interaction:

```
data["price_volume_trend"] = data["return_1"] * data["rel_volume"]
```

Liquidity proxy:

```
data["spread_pct"] = (data["ask"] - data["bid"]) / data["mid_price"]
```

High spread or low liquidity reduces expected profitability of short-term strategies.

5. Mean Reversion Features

Mean reversion assumes price deviates temporarily from equilibrium.

Z-score of price relative to rolling mean:

rolling_mean = data["price"].rolling(50).mean().shift(1)

rolling_std = data["price"].rolling(50).std().shift(1)

data["z_score"] = (data["price"] - rolling_mean) / rolling_std

- Extreme positive z-score may indicate overbought condition.
- Extreme negative z-score may indicate oversold condition.

Mean reversion works best in range-bound regimes.

6. Cross-Asset Features

Markets are interconnected.

Examples:

- Equity index vs volatility index
- Sector ETF relative strength
- Currency strength impacting export-heavy stocks

Relative strength example:

data["relative_strength"] = stock_return - index_return

Cross-asset spreads often provide regime-level information.

7. Order Book Features (Intraday)

For shorter horizons:

Order imbalance:

data["imbalance"] = (data["bid_vol"] - data["ask_vol"]) / (data["bid_vol"] + data["ask_vol"])

Spread dynamics:

data["spread_change"] = data["spread"].diff()

Short-term microstructure features decay quickly. Use appropriate sampling frequency.

8. Regime Classification Features

Some features are not predictive signals but context markers.

Examples:

- High vs low volatility regime
- Trending vs ranging market
- Risk-on vs risk-off environment

Simple trend regime:

data["trend_regime"] = (short_ma > long_ma).astype(int)

Models often perform better when conditioned on regime variables.

9. Feature Interaction and Nonlinearity

Linear models require explicit interaction terms.

Example:

*data["momentum_vol_interaction"] = data["momentum_20"] * data["volatility_20"]*

Tree-based models and neural networks can learn interactions implicitly.

However, even with nonlinear models, well-designed base features improve performance and reduce overfitting.

10. Feature Stability Testing

Before trusting a feature:

- Test performance across subperiods.
- Evaluate performance in different volatility regimes.
- Confirm economic intuition.
- Check correlation with other features.

Remove redundant features:

correlation_matrix = data.corr()

Highly correlated features inflate model complexity without adding information.

11. Avoiding Feature Overload

More features do not guarantee better performance.

Risks of too many features:

- Overfitting
- Increased variance
- Harder interpretation

- Slower training

Start simple:

- Momentum
- Volatility
- Volume
- Mean reversion
- Regime indicator
- Then expand cautiously.

12. Real-Time Constraint

Every feature must be computable live with the same logic used in backtesting.

If it requires:

- Future data
- Revised economic data
- Manual intervention

It is invalid.

Encapsulate feature generation:

```
def generate_features(data):
# compute returns
# compute momentum
# compute volatility
return feature_df
```

Use identical code in training and production.

Practical Feature Engineering Checklist

Before training:

- All rolling features are shifted.
- Features have economic rationale.
- Redundant features are removed.

- Feature stability tested across time.
- Computation matches live environment.

If a feature cannot survive these checks, remove it.

Final Principle

Feature engineering is not about mathematical creativity. It is about encoding market behavior into structured variables.

Raw price data contains noise.

Well-designed features reveal structure.

In trading systems, models amplify whatever structure you provide.

If your features encode economic reality, models can learn meaningful patterns.

If they encode noise, models will learn noise with impressive confidence.

4.3 Dimensionality Reduction and Feature Selection

Feature engineering expands your signal space. Dimensionality reduction and feature selection prevent that space from becoming a liability.

In financial modeling, more features often mean:

- Higher variance
- Greater overfitting risk
- Lower interpretability
- Slower retraining cycles

The goal is not to remove features arbitrarily. The goal is to keep only what improves generalization and robustness.

This section focuses on practical, production-oriented methods.

1. Why Too Many Features Hurt Trading Systems

Financial data has:

- Limited effective sample size
- Non-stationarity
- Regime shifts

If you have 300 features but only 3,000 daily observations, your model can easily memorize noise.

Rule of thumb:

If adding a feature improves in-sample performance dramatically but does not improve walk-forward results, it is probably capturing noise.

2. Correlation-Based Feature Pruning

The simplest method is removing highly correlated features.

Example:

```
corr_matrix = data.corr().abs()

upper = corr_matrix.where(np.triu(np.ones(corr_matrix.shape), k=1).astype(bool))

to_drop = [column for column in upper.columns if any(upper[column] > 0.9)]

data_reduced = data.drop(columns=to_drop)
```

If two features carry almost identical information, keep one.

This reduces multicollinearity and simplifies models.

However, correlation only detects linear redundancy. Nonlinear redundancy may still exist.

3. Variance Thresholding

Features with extremely low variance provide little predictive value.

Example:

from sklearn.feature_selection import VarianceThreshold

selector = VarianceThreshold(threshold=0.0001)

X_reduced = selector.fit_transform(X)

Low-variance features often represent constants or rarely changing indicators.

Removing them reduces noise.

4. Univariate Feature Selection

Evaluate each feature independently against the target.

Example using correlation with future return:

feature_scores = {}

for col in features:

feature_scores[col] = np.corrcoef(X[col], y)[0, 1]

Rank features by absolute predictive strength.

Caution:

- Univariate selection ignores interactions. Some features are weak alone but strong in combination.

Use this as a first filter, not final decision.

5. Model-Based Feature Importance

Tree-based models provide feature importance metrics.

Example with Random Forest:

model.fit(X_train, y_train)

*importance = model.feature_importances_*

Select top features:

```
important_features = X.columns[importance > threshold]
```

This captures nonlinear effects and interactions.

Better approach:

- Evaluate feature importance across rolling windows to test stability.

If importance ranking shifts drastically across time, the feature may not be robust.

6. Recursive Feature Elimination (RFE)

RFE iteratively removes least important features and retrains the model.

Example:

```
from sklearn.feature_selection import RFE

selector = RFE(model, n_features_to_select=20)

selector.fit(X_train, y_train)
```

RFE is computationally expensive but effective for moderate feature sets.

Avoid applying RFE on unstable targets without walk-forward validation.

7. Principal Component Analysis (PCA)

PCA reduces dimensionality by projecting features into orthogonal components.

Example:

```
from sklearn.decomposition import PCA

pca = PCA(n_components=10)

X_pca = pca.fit_transform(X)
```

Advantages:

- Removes multicollinearity
- Reduces dimensionality efficiently

Disadvantages:

- Components lack economic interpretation
- Harder to debug
- Sensitive to regime shifts

PCA is often useful in:

- Cross-sectional factor models
- Portfolio risk modeling
- Less ideal when interpretability matters.

8. Autoencoders (Nonlinear Reduction)

In deep learning setups, autoencoders compress features into lower-dimensional representations.

Basic structure:

- Encoder network reduces dimensionality
- Decoder reconstructs original input

Compressed representation becomes new feature set.

This method captures nonlinear relationships.

Risks:

- Overfitting
- Hidden instability
- Reduced interpretability

Use only when feature space is large and sufficiently supported by data volume.

9. Stability Testing Across Regimes

Feature selection must consider regime stability.

Procedure:

- Split data into multiple time segments.
- Train model on each segment.
- Record selected features.
- Measure overlap consistency.

If selected features vary drastically across time, the system is fragile.

Robust features remain relevant across regimes.

10. Walk-Forward Feature Validation

Never perform feature selection on the entire dataset before backtesting.

Correct procedure:

For each walk-forward window:

- Select features using training data only.
- Evaluate on validation period.
- Move window forward.
- This prevents information leakage.

Feature selection is part of the training pipeline and must be nested inside validation loops.

11. Dimensionality vs Sample Size Trade-Off

Financial datasets often have:

- High feature count
- Limited independent observations

If:

- Number of features ≈ number of observations
- The model will overfit almost certainly.

Prefer:

- Fewer, economically meaningful features
- Regularization (L1 or L2 penalties)
- Simpler architectures

Example with L1 regularization:

```
from sklearn.linear_model import Lasso
model = Lasso(alpha=0.001)
model.fit(X_train, y_train)
```

L1 encourages sparse solutions.

12. Practical Production Guidelines

Before finalizing feature set:

- Remove highly correlated features.
- Eliminate low-variance inputs.

- Validate importance stability across time.
- Perform selection inside walk-forward framework.
- Prefer interpretability when possible.
- Confirm performance survives cost assumptions.

If removing 30% of features does not significantly degrade performance, your original feature set was likely bloated.

Final Principle

Dimensionality reduction is not about compression for its own sake.

It is about:

- Reducing variance
- Improving generalization
- Enhancing robustness
- Simplifying monitoring

In trading systems, simpler models with stable features often outperform complex models with unstable feature spaces.

If feature engineering creates structure, feature selection protects it.

The objective is not maximum information.

The objective is durable, deployable signal extraction under uncertainty.

Chapter 5: Machine Learning Foundations for Trading

Machine learning in trading is where optimism meets reality. Models look brilliant in notebooks and deeply confused in live markets. I learned quickly that accuracy means very little if your predictions don't translate into better decisions.

This chapter introduces supervised and unsupervised learning techniques used in trading and explains how to evaluate models under non-stationary market conditions.

5.1 Supervised Learning for Price and Signal Prediction

Supervised learning is where most trading practitioners begin with machine learning.

- You define a target.
- You construct features.
- You train a model to map features to that target.

The difficulty is not in training the model. It is in defining the right prediction problem.

In markets, predicting price directly is often less useful than predicting a tradable outcome.

This section focuses on:

- Target definition
- Model selection
- Training pipeline
- Evaluation under market conditions

1. Defining the Prediction Target

The target determines what your model learns. Poor target design leads to useless predictions.

Regression Targets

Predict future return over horizon h:

data["future_return_5"] = data["price"].pct_change(5).shift(-5)

This creates a 5-period forward return.

Regression is useful when:

- You want magnitude prediction.
- You will scale position by predicted return.

But raw return prediction is noisy. Small forecast errors can eliminate edge after costs.

Classification Targets

Instead of predicting return magnitude, predict direction:

data["target"] = (data["future_return_5"] > 0).astype(int)

Binary classification simplifies decision-making.

Advantages:

- Robust to small magnitude errors.
- Often more stable than regression.

However, accuracy alone is meaningless. A 52% directional accuracy may be profitable—or not—depending on costs and payoff asymmetry.

Thresholded Targets

Avoid predicting tiny, non-tradable moves.

Example:

threshold = 0.002

data["target"] = np.where(

data["future_return_5"] > threshold, 1,

np.where(data["future_return_5"] < -threshold, -1, 0)

THIS CREATES THREE classes:

- Long
- Short
- No trade

This often improves economic alignment.

2. Model Selection

Model choice depends on:

- Data size
- Feature dimensionality
- Interpretability needs
- Nonlinearity of relationships
- Linear Models

Example:

```
from sklearn.linear_model import LinearRegression
model = LinearRegression()
model.fit(X_train, y_train)
```

Pros:

- Interpretable
- Low variance
- Fast retraining

Cons:

- Limited nonlinear capture

Linear models often perform surprisingly well when features are well-engineered.

Regularized Linear Models

Lasso and Ridge:

```
from sklearn.linear_model import Lasso
model = Lasso(alpha=0.001)
model.fit(X_train, y_train)
```

Regularization reduces overfitting and performs implicit feature selection.

Strong baseline for financial modeling.

Tree-Based Models

Example:

```
from sklearn.ensemble import RandomForestClassifier
model = RandomForestClassifier(n_estimators=200)
model.fit(X_train, y_train)
```

Pros:

- Capture nonlinear relationships
- Handle interactions
- Robust to scaling

Cons:

- Harder to interpret
- Can overfit if deep and unrestricted
- Gradient boosting methods are widely used in practice.

Neural Networks

Useful when:

- Large datasets exist
- Nonlinear interactions are complex
- Alternative data is involved

But:

- Require careful regularization
- Sensitive to feature scaling
- Often unstable in small datasets

Do not default to deep learning unless justified.

3. Training Pipeline

The biggest mistake in supervised learning for trading is improper validation.

Chronological Train-Test Split

- Never randomly shuffle time-series data.

Correct approach:

*split_index = int(len(data) * 0.7)*

X_train = X[:split_index]

X_test = X[split_index:]

Training must use past data only.

Walk-Forward Validation

Better approach:

- Train on window A

- Test on window B
- Slide forward
- Repeat

This simulates real deployment.

Feature selection and hyperparameter tuning must occur inside each training window.

Avoiding Leakage

Ensure:

- Rolling features are shifted.
- Targets are properly aligned.
- Scaling parameters are fit on training data only.

Example:

scaler.fit(X_train)

X_train_scaled = scaler.transform(X_train)

X_test_scaled = scaler.transform(X_test)

Never fit scaler on entire dataset.

4. Evaluation Metrics for Trading

Accuracy is not sufficient.

For classification:

- Precision
- Recall
- F1 score

But more importantly:

- Strategy return
- Sharpe ratio
- Maximum drawdown
- Profit factor

Example signal backtest logic:

```
predicted_signal = model.predict(X_test)

strategy_return = predicted_signal * actual_return
```

Evaluate cumulative performance, not just prediction accuracy.

5. Probability-Based Position Sizing

Many models output probabilities.

Instead of binary positions:

```
proba = model.predict_proba(X_test)[:, 1]

position_size = 2 * (proba - 0.5)
```

Higher confidence → larger position.

Probability calibration matters. Poor calibration leads to unstable sizing.

6. Dealing with Imbalanced Targets

Market direction may not be evenly distributed.

Example:

- 55% up days
- 45% down days

Use class weighting:

```
model = RandomForestClassifier(class_weight="balanced")
```

Or adjust loss function.

Ignoring imbalance can bias predictions toward majority class.

7. Common Failure Modes

- Overfitting due to excessive features.
- Hyperparameter tuning on full dataset.
- Ignoring transaction costs.
- Predicting too short a horizon.
- Failing to retrain as regime shifts.

Supervised learning does not adapt automatically. It must be retrained or embedded in an adaptive framework.

8. Practical Deployment Strategy

Start simple:

- Build strong baseline linear model.
- Add regularization.
- Compare with tree-based model.
- Use walk-forward evaluation.
- Incorporate cost modeling early.

If advanced models do not outperform simple baselines consistently out-of-sample, keep the simpler model.

Final Principle

Supervised learning in trading is not about maximizing predictive accuracy.

It is about converting structured features into economically meaningful signals that survive:

- Costs
- Regime changes
- Deployment latency

A model that predicts direction slightly better than chance but with disciplined risk management can be profitable.

A model with high accuracy but poor alignment to trading mechanics will fail in live markets.

Prediction is only useful if it translates into durable decision quality.

5.2 Unsupervised Learning for Regime Detection

Supervised learning predicts outcomes.
Unsupervised learning identifies structure.

In trading, the most practical use of unsupervised learning is regime detection.

Markets do not behave the same way all the time. Trend-following strategies perform well in trending regimes and fail in sideways markets. Mean-reversion works in stable conditions and collapses during breakouts.

Instead of forcing one model to fit all environments, you detect the regime first, then adapt behavior.

This section focuses on:

- What defines a market regime
- Practical unsupervised methods
- How to integrate regime detection into trading systems

1. What Is a Market Regime?

A regime is a persistent market condition characterized by:

- Volatility level
- Trend strength
- Correlation structure
- Liquidity conditions
- Risk appetite

Examples:

- High volatility / panic regime
- Low volatility / stable regime
- Strong trend regime
- Mean-reverting regime

Regimes are not labeled in real data. That is why unsupervised learning is useful.

2. Feature Selection for Regime Detection

Before clustering or modeling regimes, define regime features.

Common inputs:

- Rolling volatility
- Average return
- Trend strength
- Volume levels
- Cross-asset correlations
- Spread width

Example:

```
data["vol_20"] = data["log_return"].rolling(20).std().shift(1)
data["trend_50"] = (
data["price"].rolling(50).mean().shift(1) /
data["price"].rolling(200).mean().shift(1)
)
data["volume_ratio"] = (
data["volume"] /
data["volume"].rolling(50).mean().shift(1)
)
```

Regime features should represent structural behavior, not short-term noise.

3. K-Means Clustering

One of the simplest regime detection methods.

Example:

```
from sklearn.cluster import KMeans
X = data[["vol_20", "trend_50", "volume_ratio"]].dropna()
kmeans = KMeans(n_clusters=3, random_state=42)
data.loc[X.index, "regime"] = kmeans.fit_predict(X)
```

Each cluster represents a regime.

After clustering, analyze characteristics:

```
data.groupby("regime").mean()
```

You may discover:

- **Cluster 0** → low vol, sideways
- **Cluster 1** → high vol, downward trend
- **Cluster 2** → moderate vol, upward trend

Important:

K-means assumes spherical clusters and static structure. Markets are rarely that simple.

4. Gaussian Mixture Models (GMM)

GMM provides probabilistic regime membership.

Example:

```
from sklearn.mixture import GaussianMixture

gmm = GaussianMixture(n_components=3)

data["regime"] = gmm.fit_predict(X)
```

Advantages:

- Soft assignment (probability of each regime)
- More flexible cluster shapes

This allows position scaling based on regime probability.

Example:

```
regime_prob = gmm.predict_proba(X)
```

Higher confidence in high-volatility regime → reduce risk.

5. Hidden Markov Models (HMM)

HMMs are particularly useful for time-series regime modeling.

They assume:

- Hidden states (regimes)
- Observed data generated by those states
- State transitions over time

This introduces temporal persistence.

Conceptually:

- **State 1:** Low volatility
- **State 2:** High volatility

Transition probabilities define how likely regime shifts occur

HMMs better reflect real market behavior because regimes persist rather than jump randomly.

6. Regime Stability and Validation

Unsupervised learning always produces clusters—even if no real structure exists.

Validation is essential.

Steps:

- Visualize regimes on price chart.
- Compare volatility across clusters.
- Evaluate transition frequency.
- Check economic interpretation.

If regimes change every few days, clustering may be capturing noise.

Regimes should be persistent enough to justify adaptive strategies.

7. Integrating Regime Detection into Trading Systems

Regime detection should not trade directly. It should modify strategy behavior.

Example 1: Strategy Switching

if regime == 0:

signal = momentum_signal

elif regime == 1:

signal = mean_reversion_signal

Different strategies activated depending on environment.

Example 2: Risk Adjustment

if regime == high_vol_regime:

*position_size *= 0.5*

Risk control becomes regime-aware.

Example 3: Feature Conditioning

Add regime label as additional feature:

X["regime"] = data["regime"]

Supervised model learns conditional behavior.

8. Rolling Recalibration

Regimes evolve. Clusters defined over 10 years may not reflect current dynamics.

Use rolling retraining:

if new_month:

kmeans.fit(recent_regime_data)

However, avoid excessive recalibration. Too frequent updates introduce instability.

9. Common Pitfalls

- Over-clustering (too many regimes).
- Using short windows that capture noise.
- Ignoring economic meaning.
- Failing to test strategy performance within each regime.

If regime detection does not improve strategy stability or risk-adjusted returns, it adds unnecessary complexity.

10. When Unsupervised Learning Adds Real Value

Most useful when:

- Strategy performance is highly regime-dependent
- Volatility shifts dramatically
- Cross-asset correlations fluctuate
- Portfolio allocation decisions depend on macro state

Less useful when:

- Strategy operates at ultra-short horizons
- Market behavior is structurally stable

Final Principle

Unsupervised learning does not predict price.

It reveals structure in market behavior.

Regime detection allows your system to ask:

- *"What kind of market am I in right now?"*

Instead of forcing one static model to survive all conditions, you allow behavior to adapt to structural shifts.

In practice, regime awareness improves:

- Risk control
- Strategy selection
- Capital allocation

Used carefully, it increases robustness.

Used blindly, it adds noise disguised as structure.

The objective is not to label markets perfectly.

It is to reduce vulnerability to structural change.

5.3 Model Evaluation Metrics for Financial Data

A model that scores 60% accuracy can lose money.
A model with 52% accuracy can generate strong risk-adjusted returns.

Financial model evaluation is different from standard machine learning evaluation because prediction quality is not the final objective. Economic performance is.

This section focuses on how to evaluate models in a way that reflects trading reality.

We will cover:

- Statistical prediction metrics
- Trading performance metrics
- Risk-adjusted evaluation
- Stability and robustness testing

1. Prediction Metrics: Necessary but Not Sufficient

These metrics evaluate how well the model predicts the target variable.

Accuracy (Classification)

accuracy = (y_pred == y_true).mean()

Accuracy is misleading in finance.

If 55% of days are positive returns, predicting "up" every day gives 55% accuracy. That does not imply profitability.

Use accuracy only as a preliminary indicator.

Precision and Recall

Precision:

precision = true_positives / predicted_positives

RECALL:

recall = true_positives / actual_positives

- Precision measures signal quality.
- Recall measures signal coverage.

In trading, high precision often matters more than high recall. You prefer fewer but higher-quality trades.

F1 Score

Balances precision and recall.

*f1 = 2 * (precision * recall) / (precision + recall)*

Still insufficient alone, because none of these metrics account for return magnitude or transaction costs.

Mean Squared Error (Regression)

*mse = ((y_true - y_pred) ** 2).mean()*

Lower MSE does not necessarily imply better trading outcomes.

Small magnitude errors near zero can still flip trade direction.

2. Translating Predictions into Strategy Returns

Ultimately, you must convert predictions into trades.

Example:

*strategy_return = y_pred * actual_return*

If classification:

*strategy_return = np.sign(y_pred) * actual_return*

From here, evaluation shifts from ML metrics to financial metrics.

3. Return-Based Metrics

Cumulative Return

cumulative_return = (1 + strategy_return).cumprod() - 1

Measures total growth over evaluation period.

However, cumulative return ignores risk.

Average Return Per Trade

Useful for high-frequency strategies.

avg_trade_return = strategy_return[strategy_return != 0].mean()

Must exceed average transaction cost.

4. Risk-Adjusted Metrics

Sharpe Ratio

Most common metric in finance.

```
sharpe = strategy_return.mean() / strategy_return.std()
```

Annualized version:

```
sharpe_annual = sharpe * np.sqrt(periods_per_year)
```

Sharpe measures return per unit of volatility.

Limitations:

- Assumes normal distribution
- Penalizes upside volatility equally
- Sensitive to outliers

Still widely used as baseline.

Sortino Ratio

Focuses only on downside volatility.

```
downside_std = strategy_return[strategy_return < 0].std()

sortino = strategy_return.mean() / downside_std
```

Better for asymmetric strategies.

Maximum Drawdown

Largest peak-to-trough decline.

```
cum_returns = (1 + strategy_return).cumprod()

rolling_max = cum_returns.cummax()

drawdown = cum_returns / rolling_max - 1

max_drawdown = drawdown.min()
```

Drawdown reflects psychological and capital risk.

A strategy with high Sharpe but deep drawdowns may be impractical.

Calmar Ratio

Return divided by maximum drawdown.

```
calmar = annual_return / abs(max_drawdown)
```

Useful for evaluating capital efficiency.

5. Classification-Specific Financial Metrics

Hit Ratio

Percentage of profitable trades.

hit_ratio = (strategy_return > 0).mean()

High hit ratio does not guarantee profitability if losses are large.

Profit Factor

Ratio of gross profits to gross losses.

*profit_factor = strategy_return[strategy_return > 0].sum() / *

abs(strategy_return[strategy_return < 0].sum())

Profit factor > 1 indicates profitability.

More informative than accuracy for trading.

6. Cost-Aware Evaluation

Always subtract:

- Commission
- Spread
- Slippage
- Market impact

Adjusted return:

net_return = gross_return - transaction_cost

A strategy that ignores costs is not deployable.

Cost sensitivity analysis:

- Increase assumed cost by 25%
- Increase by 50%
- Test robustness

If performance collapses under minor cost changes, edge is weak.

7. Stability Across Time

Performance must be consistent.

Split evaluation period into subperiods:

subperiod_results = []

Compare Sharpe, drawdown, return across:

- Bull markets
- Bear markets
- High volatility periods
- Low volatility periods

If performance is concentrated in one short window, strategy is fragile.

8. Walk-Forward Evaluation

Proper evaluation requires:

- Train on historical window
- Test on next window
- Slide forward
- Aggregate results

Do not evaluate on entire dataset at once.

Walk-forward performance approximates live deployment behavior.

9. Statistical Significance

Even profitable backtests may be statistical noise.

Estimate:

- Confidence intervals of Sharpe
- Bootstrapped performance
- Monte Carlo simulations

Example bootstrap:

bootstrapped_returns = np.random.choice(strategy_return, size=len(strategy_return), replace=True)

Assess variability in Sharpe across simulations.

If Sharpe collapses under resampling, robustness is questionable.

10. Degradation Monitoring

Model evaluation does not end at deployment.

Track:

- Rolling Sharpe
- Rolling drawdown
- Prediction accuracy drift

Example:

*rolling_sharpe = strategy_return.rolling(252).mean() / *

strategy_return.rolling(252).std()

Declining rolling performance may indicate regime shift or model decay.

Practical Evaluation Checklist

Before approving a model:

- Statistical metrics reviewed.
- Net returns after costs calculated.
- Sharpe and drawdown evaluated.
- Performance stable across subperiods.
- Walk-forward results consistent.
- Sensitivity to cost changes tested.
- Bootstrapped variability assessed.

If performance depends on a single favorable assumption, reject or redesign.

Final Principle

In financial modeling, prediction accuracy is secondary.

The primary objective is risk-adjusted profitability under realistic constraints.

A good model:

- Survives transaction costs
- Maintains stable risk profile
- Degrades gradually across regimes
- Performs consistently out-of-sample

Evaluation is not about finding the highest metric.

It is about determining whether the edge is durable, deployable, and economically meaningful.

Chapter 6: Deep Learning Models in Trading

Deep learning feels like magic—until it memorizes noise and confidently loses money. I've built neural networks that learned everything except how to survive. Power without restraint is dangerous, especially when markets constantly change.

This chapter covers neural networks, CNNs, and transformer-based approaches for financial data, emphasizing regularization, robustness, and realistic expectations.

6.1 Neural Networks for Time-Series Forecasting

Neural networks are powerful function approximators. In trading, that power can either uncover nonlinear structure—or memorize noise with confidence.

Before using neural networks for financial time-series forecasting, you must understand two constraints:

- Financial time series are noisy and non-stationary.
- Data volume is often smaller than in typical deep learning domains.
- Neural networks can work in trading, but only when applied with discipline.
- This section focuses on practical implementation for price and signal forecasting.

1. Why Use Neural Networks in Trading?

Traditional linear models assume linear relationships between features and returns. Markets often exhibit:

- Nonlinear interactions
- Conditional behavior (signal works only in certain regimes)
- Feature cross-effects

Neural networks can capture:

- Nonlinear dependencies
- Interaction effects
- Hierarchical feature combinations

However, they do not create signal. They amplify the structure already present in your features.

2. Preparing Time-Series Data for Neural Networks

Neural networks require structured input tensors.

For time-series forecasting, use sliding windows.

Example: using past 20 timesteps to predict next return.

```
import numpy as np

window_size = 20

X = []
```

```
y = []
for i in range(window_size, len(data) - 1):
X.append(data.iloc[i-window_size:i].values)
y.append(data["future_return"].iloc[i])
X = np.array(X)
y = np.array(y)
```

Input shape:

- (samples, timesteps, features)

Always ensure:

- No future leakage
- Proper alignment of target

3. Feedforward Neural Networks (MLP)

Simplest neural network architecture.

Flatten time window:

```
X_flat = X.reshape(X.shape[0], -1)
```

Model example (using Keras-like pseudocode):

```
model = Sequential()
model.add(Dense(64, activation='relu', input_dim=X_flat.shape[1]))
model.add(Dense(32, activation='relu'))
model.add(Dense(1))
model.compile(optimizer='adam', loss='mse')
```

Pros:

- Easy to implement
- Good baseline
- Works well with engineered features

Cons:

- Does not explicitly model temporal structure

Often effective when features already encode temporal information.

4. Recurrent Neural Networks (RNN)

RNNs process sequences step by step.

However, vanilla RNNs struggle with long dependencies and gradient instability.

More practical variants:

- **LSTM** (Long Short-Term Memory)
- **GRU** (Gated Recurrent Unit)

Example:

```
model = Sequential()

model.add(LSTM(64, input_shape=(window_size, num_features)))

model.add(Dense(1))

model.compile(optimizer='adam', loss='mse')
```

Advantages:

- Captures sequential dependencies
- Maintains memory state

Limitations:

- Computationally heavier
- Prone to overfitting
- May not outperform simpler models in noisy data

5. Convolutional Neural Networks (1D CNN)

1D CNNs can extract local temporal patterns.

Example:

```
model = Sequential()

model.add(Conv1D(filters=32, kernel_size=3, activation='relu',

input_shape=(window_size, num_features)))

model.add(GlobalMaxPooling1D())

model.add(Dense(1))
```

model.compile(optimizer='adam', loss='mse')

CNN advantages:

- Efficient
- Capture short-term patterns
- Less prone to overfitting than deep RNN stacks

Often strong performers in financial forecasting.

6. Regularization Is Not Optional

Neural networks easily overfit financial data.

Use:

- Dropout
- L2 regularization
- Early stopping

Example:

model.add(Dropout(0.3))

Early stopping:

EarlyStopping(monitor='val_loss', patience=5)

Always maintain a separate validation set.

If validation performance diverges from training performance, reduce model complexity.

7. Scaling and Normalization

Neural networks are sensitive to input scale.

Normalize features:

from sklearn.preprocessing import StandardScaler

scaler = StandardScaler()

X_train_scaled = scaler.fit_transform(X_train)

X_test_scaled = scaler.transform(X_test)

For sequence data, scale features before window construction.

Never fit scaler on entire dataset.

8. Loss Functions and Targets

For regression:

loss = 'mse'

For classification:

loss = 'binary_crossentropy'

But trading-specific improvement comes from aligning target to economic outcome.

Example: predicting sign of return above threshold instead of raw return.

9. Evaluation in Trading Context

After training:

predictions = model.predict(X_test)

*strategy_return = predictions.flatten() * actual_returns*

Evaluate:

- Sharpe ratio
- Maximum drawdown
- Stability across subperiods

Neural networks must outperform simpler baselines consistently to justify added complexity.

If performance gain is marginal, prefer simpler model.

10. Common Failure Modes

- Too many layers relative to dataset size.
- Training on entire dataset before splitting.
- Ignoring regime shifts.
- Over-optimizing hyperparameters.
- Ignoring transaction costs.

Deep models can show impressive in-sample performance while failing immediately in live markets.

11. When Neural Networks Make Sense

Neural networks are more justified when:

- Large multi-asset dataset exists.

- Many nonlinear interactions are suspected.
- Alternative data (text, sentiment) is included.
- Signal structure is complex and conditional.

Less justified when:

- Dataset is small.
- Strategy horizon is long-term and stable.
- Features are already linear and interpretable.

Practical Deployment Strategy

Start with:

- Regularized linear baseline.
- Tree-based model comparison.
- Simple MLP.
- Then LSTM or CNN if justified.
- Escalate complexity gradually.

Track incremental improvement at each step.

If neural network does not significantly improve risk-adjusted performance in walk-forward evaluation, do not deploy it.

Final Principle

Neural networks do not understand markets. They approximate functions.

Their success depends entirely on:

- Data integrity
- Feature quality
- Regularization discipline
- Proper validation

In trading, complexity must be earned.

A neural network is valuable only if it produces stable, deployable improvement—not impressive training curves.

6.2 CNNs and Transformers for Market Pattern Recognition

Traditional models treat features as independent inputs.

CNNs and Transformers treat data as structured sequences.

In financial markets, structure matters:

- Price evolves sequentially.
- Order flow contains local patterns.
- Volatility clusters over time.
- Cross-asset relationships shift conditionally.

CNNs and Transformers are designed to detect patterns within structured data. Used correctly, they can extract temporal and cross-sectional structure that simpler models miss.

Used carelessly, they memorize noise at scale.

This section focuses on practical application in trading systems.

1. Convolutional Neural Networks (CNNs) for Time-Series

CNNs are not only for images. A 1D CNN can detect short-term temporal patterns in price or order flow data.

Why CNNs Work in Financial Data

CNNs:

- Capture local dependencies (e.g., 3–10 timestep patterns)
- Share weights across time
- Are computationally efficient
- Require fewer parameters than deep recurrent networks

For short-horizon trading, local structure often matters more than long-term memory.

Example: 1D CNN for Price Sequences

Input shape:

- (samples, timesteps, features)

Example model:

```
from tensorflow.keras.models import Sequential
from tensorflow.keras.layers import Conv1D, GlobalAveragePooling1D, Dense
model = Sequential()
model.add(Conv1D(filters=32, kernel_size=3, activation='relu',
input_shape=(window_size, num_features)))
model.add(GlobalAveragePooling1D())
model.add(Dense(1))
model.compile(optimizer='adam', loss='mse')
```

Kernel size controls how many timesteps are examined at once.

Smaller kernel:

- Captures short bursts

Larger kernel:

- Captures broader short-term trends

CNN for Order Book Data

For Level 2 order book:

Features might include:

- Bid volumes across levels
- Ask volumes across levels
- Spread
- Imbalance

Reshape as:

- (timesteps, price_levels × features)

CNNs can detect:

- Liquidity shifts
- Order clustering
- Pressure buildup patterns

This is common in intraday and market-making research.

2. Multi-Channel CNNs

You can treat different feature groups as separate channels.

Example:

- **Channel 1:** Price features
- **Channel 2:** Volume features
- **Channel 3:** Order imbalance

CNN processes them jointly.

This allows structured feature learning instead of manual interaction engineering.

3. Transformers for Financial Time-Series

Transformers were designed for natural language processing, but their attention mechanism works well for sequential financial data.

Core idea:

- Instead of processing sequence step-by-step (like RNNs), Transformers use self-attention to weigh the importance of all past timesteps simultaneously.

Why Transformers Can Be Useful

Markets are not purely local in memory.

Example:

- A volatility spike 30 days ago may influence current behavior.
- Macro event memory may persist longer than fixed window CNN captures.

Self-attention allows the model to focus dynamically on relevant historical points.

Conceptual Transformer Block

Key components:

- Multi-head attention
- Feedforward network
- Positional encoding

Pseudocode structure:

```
model = TransformerModel(
input_dim=num_features,
num_heads=4,
num_layers=2,
hidden_dim=64
)
```

(Implementation details vary by framework.)

4. Positional Encoding in Financial Data

Transformers do not inherently know order. You must encode position.

For financial time series:

- Add timestep index encoding.
- Use sinusoidal positional encodings.
- Or learn positional embeddings.

Without positional encoding, sequence order information is lost.

5. When CNNs vs Transformers Make Sense

CNNs

Best for:

- Short-term pattern detection
- Intraday strategies
- Order book modeling
- Limited data environments

Advantages:

- Efficient
- Lower parameter count
- Easier to regularize
- Transformers

Best for:

- Medium-to-long horizon forecasting
- Cross-asset modeling
- Regime-sensitive learning
- Large datasets

Advantages:

- Flexible dependency modeling
- Dynamic attention weighting

Disadvantages:

- High parameter count
- Greater overfitting risk
- Heavy computational cost

6. Regularization and Data Constraints

Financial datasets are smaller than NLP datasets.

Transformers can easily overfit.

Apply:

- Dropout
- Weight decay
- Early stopping
- Reduced model depth

Example regularization:

optimizer = Adam(learning_rate=1e-4)

Lower learning rates reduce instability.

7. Evaluation Beyond Training Loss

Do not evaluate CNNs or Transformers using training metrics alone.

After prediction:

pred = model.predict(X_test)

*strategy_return = pred.flatten() * actual_return*

Evaluate:

- Sharpe ratio
- Drawdown
- Regime stability
- Turnover

Deep architectures must justify complexity by producing materially better out-of-sample results.

8. Multi-Asset and Cross-Sectional Transformers

Advanced setups use Transformers to model relationships across assets.

Input:

- Matrix of assets × features over time.

Attention mechanism can learn:

- Correlation shifts
- Sector clustering
- Risk contagion patterns

This is particularly useful for portfolio allocation tasks.

9. Common Failure Modes

- Excessive model size relative to data volume.
- Ignoring transaction costs in evaluation.
- Using long sequences without meaningful signal.
- Hyperparameter over-optimization.
- Lack of walk-forward validation.

Deep models amplify noise if signal-to-noise ratio is low.

10. Practical Deployment Strategy

Stepwise progression:

- Start with linear or tree baseline.
- Test simple MLP.

- Introduce CNN for short-term sequence modeling.
- Only use Transformers if clear evidence supports long-range dependency modeling.

Always compare:

- Out-of-sample Sharpe
- Drawdown behavior
- Stability across regimes

If improvement is marginal or unstable, revert to simpler architecture.

Final Principle

CNNs detect local patterns.

Transformers detect global dependencies.

Both can enhance pattern recognition in financial time-series.

But neither creates signal from noise.

Deep architectures are tools for extracting structured relationships when they genuinely exist.

In trading systems, complexity must be supported by:

- Sufficient data
- Clear validation
- Economic intuition
- Stable out-of-sample performance

If those conditions are not met, deeper models simply overfit faster.

6.3 Overfitting, Regularization, and Model Robustness

In trading, overfitting is not a possibility. It is the default outcome.

Financial data is:

- Noisy
- Non-stationary
- Low signal-to-noise
- Structurally unstable

If your model looks excellent in-sample, you should assume it is overfitted until proven otherwise.

This section focuses on:

- Why overfitting is especially severe in trading
- Practical regularization techniques
- Robustness testing before deployment

1. Why Overfitting Is Worse in Financial Markets

In many ML domains (vision, language), signal is strong and persistent.

In financial markets:

- Signal is weak
- Regimes shift
- Competition adapts
- Noise dominates

A deep model with thousands of parameters can easily fit randomness.

Symptoms of overfitting:

- Very high training performance
- Large drop in validation performance
- Sensitivity to small hyperparameter changes
- Performance concentrated in one short time window

In trading, the cost of overfitting is capital loss—not just lower accuracy.

2. Sources of Overfitting in Trading Systems

Common causes:

- Too many features relative to data size
- Excessively complex models
- Over-optimized hyperparameters
- Data leakage
- Repeated backtest tuning

Each iteration of strategy tweaking increases risk of implicit data mining.

Even manual parameter adjustments based on backtest charts can introduce bias.

3. Regularization Techniques

Regularization reduces model complexity and prevents memorization of noise.

L1 and L2 Regularization

L1 (Lasso) encourages sparsity:

```
from sklearn.linear_model import Lasso
model = Lasso(alpha=0.001)
```

L2 (Ridge) penalizes large coefficients:

```
from sklearn.linear_model import Ridge
model = Ridge(alpha=1.0)
```

These are effective for linear and shallow models.

Dropout (Neural Networks)

Randomly disables neurons during training:

```
model.add(Dropout(0.3))
```

Prevents co-adaptation of features.

Use moderately (e.g., 0.2–0.5). Excessive dropout harms learning.

Early Stopping

Stop training when validation performance stops improving.

EarlyStopping(monitor='val_loss', patience=5)

Prevents over-training.

Model Size Reduction

Often the best regularization is simplification.

Reduce:

- Number of layers
- Number of neurons
- Tree depth
- Feature count

If reducing complexity barely affects out-of-sample performance, original model was over-parameterized.

4. Cross-Validation for Time-Series

Standard k-fold cross-validation is invalid for time-series.

Use walk-forward validation:

- Train on window A
- Validate on window B
- Move forward
- Repeat

Evaluate aggregated performance across windows.

Consistency across multiple periods is more important than peak performance in one period.

5. Out-of-Sample Discipline

Divide data into:

- Training
- Validation
- Final holdout test

The holdout test must remain untouched until final evaluation.

If you repeatedly test and adjust based on holdout results, it becomes part of training.

Preserve one untouched evaluation window for final verification.

6. Sensitivity Analysis

Robust models are stable under small perturbations.

Test:

- Slight changes in hyperparameters
- Slight changes in training window
- Slight increase in transaction cost
- Slight latency increase

If performance collapses under small changes, strategy is fragile.

Example:

- Increase assumed cost by 25%.

If Sharpe drops from 1.5 to 0.2, edge is likely marginal.

7. Parameter Stability Across Time

For linear models, track coefficient stability.

Example:

- Train model on rolling windows and compare coefficients.

If coefficients flip signs frequently, model may be unstable.

For tree-based models, track feature importance across windows.

Stable importance signals more durable relationships.

8. Monte Carlo and Bootstrap Testing

Resample returns to evaluate variability.

boot_returns = np.random.choice(strategy_return,

size=len(strategy_return),

replace=True)

Recompute Sharpe and drawdown multiple times.

Wide dispersion implies unstable performance.

Monte Carlo also helps simulate:

- Different trade ordering

- Randomized slippage
- Execution noise

Robust strategies degrade gradually, not catastrophically.

9. Stress Testing Across Regimes

Explicitly evaluate performance in:

- High volatility periods
- Low volatility periods
- Bull markets
- Bear markets

A strategy that performs well only in one regime is not robust.

Use regime segmentation from previous chapter to test conditional performance.

10. Turnover and Overfitting

High turnover strategies are more sensitive to overfitting.

Small predictive errors become expensive after costs.

Monitor:

turnover = abs(position.diff()).sum()

If performance depends on extremely frequent trading with thin margins, overfitting risk is high.

11. Simplicity as a Robustness Tool

Often, simpler models:

- Generalize better
- Require fewer assumptions
- Are easier to monitor
- Degrade more gracefully

Complex architectures must justify themselves with clear and stable improvement.

If performance gain is marginal, choose simplicity.

12. Deployment Readiness Checklist

Before deploying:

- Walk-forward performance stable.
- Cost sensitivity tested.
- Hyperparameters not excessively tuned.
- Feature importance stable across time.
- Holdout dataset confirms results.
- Monte Carlo tests show acceptable dispersion.

If any of these fail, revisit model complexity.

Final Principle

Overfitting is not eliminated by using advanced models.

It is reduced through:

- Discipline
- Simplicity
- Conservative validation
- Continuous monitoring

In trading, robustness matters more than peak performance.

A slightly lower Sharpe that survives regime shifts is more valuable than a high Sharpe that collapses in live markets.

Models do not fail because they are not smart enough.

They fail because they were trained to fit the past too perfectly.

Chapter 7: Reinforcement Learning for Trading Agents

This is where things get exciting—and dangerous. Teaching an agent to act instead of predict feels like giving it independence. I also learned that poorly designed reward functions can teach agents some truly impressive ways to lose money creatively.

This chapter explains reinforcement learning concepts, environment design, reward shaping, and the unique challenges of applying RL to financial markets.

7.1 Markov Decision Processes and Reward Design

Reinforcement learning (RL) reframes trading from prediction to decision-making.

Instead of asking:

- What will price do next?

We ask:

- Given current conditions, what action should I take to maximize long-term objective?

The formal framework behind this is the Markov Decision Process (MDP).

If you misunderstand the MDP structure or design the reward incorrectly, your agent will learn behaviors that look intelligent but lose money.

This section focuses on:

- The structure of MDPs in trading
- State, action, and transition modeling
- Reward design aligned with financial objectives

1. Markov Decision Process in Trading

An MDP is defined by:

- **State** (S)
- **Action** (A)
- **Transition dynamics** (P)
- **Reward function** (R)
- **Discount factor** (γ)

In trading terms:

- **State** = market and portfolio information
- **Action** = trading decision
- **Transition** = how market evolves and portfolio changes
- **Reward** = financial outcome of action

1.1 State Definition

The state must summarize all relevant information available at time t.

Example state structure:

state = {

"returns": last_n_returns,

"volatility": current_vol,

"position": current_inventory,

"cash": available_cash,

"drawdown": current_drawdown,

"spread": current_spread

}

Key principle:

State must only include information available at decision time.

- **Too little information** → poor decisions.
- **Too much irrelevant information** → overfitting and instability.

1.2 Action Space

Actions define what the agent can do.

Common action representations:

Discrete:

- **0** → Hold
- **1** → Buy
- **2** → Sell

Example:

actions = ["hold", "buy", "sell"]

Continuous:

- Position size between -1 and 1
- Allocation weight

Example:

action = model_output # value between -1 and 1

Discrete actions simplify learning. Continuous actions allow finer control but increase complexity.

1.3 Transition Dynamics

In trading, transition dynamics are partially stochastic and unknown.

After taking action:

- Market price evolves
- Portfolio value changes
- Risk exposure shifts

Unlike games, the environment is not fully controllable.

Your agent influences price only indirectly through market impact.

2. The Markov Property in Financial Markets

An MDP assumes:

- *The future depends only on the current state, not full history.*

In reality, markets are not strictly Markovian. However, if your state captures sufficient recent information (e.g., rolling windows, volatility, regime indicators), the Markov approximation becomes reasonable.

Window-based state example:

state = data.iloc[t-window_size:t]

Proper state construction is critical. Poor state design cannot be fixed by algorithm choice.

3. Reward Design: The Most Critical Component

Reward defines what the agent optimizes.

If reward is poorly designed, the agent will exploit loopholes.

This is the most common failure in RL trading systems.

3.1 Naive Reward: Raw PnL

Simple reward:

reward = current_portfolio_value - previous_portfolio_value

Problem:

- Encourages excessive risk
- Ignores volatility
- Ignores transaction costs
- Ignores drawdown

The agent may learn to take extreme positions.

3.2 Cost-Aware Reward

Include transaction costs:

reward = pnl - transaction_cost

Transaction cost may include:

- Spread
- Commission
- Slippage

Without cost modeling, RL agents overtrade aggressively.

3.3 Risk-Adjusted Reward

Incorporate volatility penalty:

*reward = pnl - lambda_risk * volatility*

Or penalize drawdowns:

*reward = pnl - lambda_dd * max(0, current_drawdown)*

This encourages smoother equity curves.

3.4 Inventory Penalty (Market Making)

For inventory-sensitive strategies:

*reward = pnl - lambda_inventory * abs(position)*

Prevents excessive directional exposure.

3.5 Sharpe-Oriented Reward (Approximate)

You can approximate risk-adjusted return:

reward = pnl / (rolling_volatility + 1e-6)

Be cautious: unstable denominators create noise.

Often better to optimize incremental reward and evaluate Sharpe externally.

4. Discount Factor (γ)

Discount factor determines how much future rewards matter.

- **γ close to 0** → short-term focus
- **γ close to 1** → long-term optimization
- Short-horizon intraday strategies may use lower γ.
- Portfolio allocation tasks may require higher γ.

Choosing γ incorrectly changes behavior significantly.

5. Reward Hacking Risk

Agents optimize reward mathematically, not economically.

Common reward hacking behaviors:

- Exploiting unrealistic execution assumptions
- Overtrading in low-cost simulation
- Taking extreme leverage
- Holding positions indefinitely to avoid realized loss

Guardrails must be hard-coded:

if drawdown > max_limit:

terminate_episode()

Constraints should not be learned. They should be enforced.

6. Episode Design

An episode may represent:

- One trading day
- One month
- Entire backtest period

Short episodes:

- Faster training
- May encourage short-term behavior

Long episodes:

- Better long-term optimization
- Slower convergence

Choose episode structure aligned with strategy horizon.

7. Practical MDP Design Checklist

Before training:

- State includes only observable, timely data.
- Actions are realistic given liquidity.
- Transaction costs are included.
- Risk constraints are hard-coded.
- Reward aligns with real financial objective.
- Episode structure matches strategy timeframe.

If reward and constraints are misaligned, no RL algorithm will fix it.

Final Principle

In reinforcement learning for trading:

- The algorithm is secondary.
- The MDP design is primary.
- State defines what the agent sees.
- Action defines what it can control.
- Reward defines what it learns to value.

If reward prioritizes short-term gains without risk control, the agent will behave aggressively.

If reward balances profit, cost, and risk, the agent can learn disciplined behavior.

In trading systems, reward design is not a detail.

It is the economic definition of intelligence.

7.2 Policy-Based and Value-Based Methods

Once your trading problem is framed as a Markov Decision Process, the next question is:

- How should the agent learn to act?

Reinforcement learning methods generally fall into two categories:

- Value-based methods
- Policy-based methods

There are also hybrid approaches that combine both.

The choice affects stability, action flexibility, and suitability for financial markets.

1. Value-Based Methods

Value-based methods learn a function that estimates the value of taking an action in a given state.

Formally:

$$Q(s, a) = \text{expected cumulative reward from state } s \text{ taking action } a$$

The agent then selects the action with the highest estimated value.

1.1 Q-Learning (Conceptual Overview)

Basic idea:

1. Observe state s
2. Take action a
3. Receive reward r
4. Update Q-value estimate

Update rule (simplified):

$$Q(s, a) \leftarrow Q(s, a) + \alpha\left[r + \gamma \max_a Q(s', a) - Q(s, a)\right]$$

In trading terms:

- s = market + portfolio state
- a = buy / sell / hold
- r = cost-adjusted PnL
- s' = next market state

1.2 Deep Q-Networks (DQN)

When state space is large, Q-values are approximated using neural networks.

Pseudo-structure:

q_values = model(state)

action = np.argmax(q_values)

Advantages:

- Simple action selection
- Works well with discrete actions
- Relatively stable for small action spaces

Limitations in trading:

- Discrete action constraint (e.g., buy/sell/hold only)
- Struggles with continuous position sizing
- Sensitive to reward noise

DQN is more suitable for:

- Directional trading with fixed position size
- Simplified decision frameworks

2. Policy-Based Methods

Policy-based methods learn the policy directly.

Instead of learning Q-values, they learn:

$$\pi(a|s) = \text{probability of action given state}$$

The model outputs actions directly.

2.1 Basic Policy Gradient

The agent:

- Samples actions from policy
- Observes reward
- Adjusts parameters to increase probability of profitable actions

Example conceptual structure:

action_probs = policy_model(state)

action = sample(action_probs)

Advantages:

- Naturally handles stochastic policies
- Supports continuous action spaces
- More flexible for position sizing

Limitations:

- Higher variance in training
- Sensitive to noisy reward

2.2 Continuous Action Spaces

For trading, continuous action space is often more realistic:

Action example:

- Position size between -1 and +1
- Allocation weight

Policy network output:

action = policy_model(state) # continuous value

This allows:

- Fine-grained capital allocation
- Dynamic scaling
- Risk-sensitive behavior

Value-based methods struggle with this unless discretized.

3. Actor-Critic Methods (Hybrid)

Actor-Critic combines:

- **Actor** → policy function
- **Critic** → value estimator

The critic evaluates how good the actor's decisions are.

This reduces variance and improves stability.

Conceptual structure:

value_estimate = critic(state)

action = actor(state)

POPULAR VARIANTS:

- **A2C** (Advantage Actor-Critic)
- **PPO** (Proximal Policy Optimization)
- **DDPG** (Deep Deterministic Policy Gradient)

In financial applications, PPO and actor-critic methods are commonly used due to improved stability.

4. Choosing Between Value-Based and Policy-Based in Trading

When Value-Based Methods Make Sense

- Discrete actions (buy/sell/hold)
- Small state space
- Simplified trading environment
- Limited computational budget

Use case:

- Directional trading with fixed position sizes.

When Policy-Based Methods Make Sense

- Continuous position sizing

- Portfolio allocation problems
- Multi-asset optimization
- Risk-sensitive trading

Use case:

- Dynamic capital allocation or execution control.

5. Exploration vs Exploitation

RL requires exploration.

In trading, exploration can be expensive.

Common exploration methods:

- Epsilon-greedy (value-based)
- Stochastic policy sampling (policy-based)

Example epsilon-greedy:

```
if random.random() < epsilon:
action = random_action()
else:
action = greedy_action()
```

In live trading, exploration must be carefully limited or performed in simulation only.

Production systems often reduce exploration significantly after training.

6. Stability Challenges in Financial Markets

Financial environments are:

- Non-stationary
- Partially observable
- Low signal-to-noise

Value-based methods may:

- Overestimate Q-values
- Become unstable with noisy rewards

Policy-based methods may:

- Overreact to short-term reward fluctuations
- Require careful tuning

Hybrid methods often provide better trade-offs.

7. Practical Training Considerations

Regardless of method:

- Include transaction costs in reward.
- Limit leverage through hard constraints.
- Use replay buffers carefully (avoid mixing distant regimes excessively).
- Train on rolling windows to simulate non-stationarity.

Evaluate policy via walk-forward testing.

Never rely solely on cumulative reward during training.

8. Risk Constraints Outside the Learning Loop

Critical rule:

Risk limits must not be learned.

Hard constraints example:

if position_size > max_position:

position_size = max_position

Agent autonomy should operate inside strict capital boundaries.

Final Principle

- Value-based methods estimate how good actions are.
- Policy-based methods learn how to act directly.
- Actor-critic methods combine both.

In trading systems:

- Use value-based methods for simple, discrete decision problems.
- Use policy-based or actor-critic methods for continuous allocation and adaptive sizing.

The algorithm choice matters.

But stability, reward alignment, and risk constraints matter more.

In financial markets, reinforcement learning does not fail because the method is weak.

It fails because the environment is noisy and the reward is poorly designed.

7.3 Challenges of Reinforcement Learning in Markets

Reinforcement learning is conceptually appealing for trading:

- It optimizes long-term reward.
- It adapts through feedback.
- It makes sequential decisions.

On paper, financial markets look like ideal RL environments.

In practice, they are one of the most difficult environments for RL.

This section focuses on the structural challenges that make reinforcement learning in markets uniquely hard.

1. Low Signal-to-Noise Ratio

Markets are noisy.

Price movement is driven by:

- Random order flow
- News shocks
- Liquidity imbalances
- Institutional flows
- Macro events

The true predictive signal is often weak.

RL depends on reward feedback to update policy. When reward is dominated by noise, learning becomes unstable.

Effect:

- High variance in updates
- Slow convergence
- Overfitting to random fluctuations

In many cases, simpler supervised methods outperform RL because the environment does not provide a strong enough signal for long-horizon learning.

2. Non-Stationarity

The environment changes over time.

- Volatility regimes shift
- Correlations break
- Liquidity conditions evolve
- Regulation changes
- Market participants adapt
- In games like chess, the rules do not change.
- In markets, the "rules" evolve continuously.

An RL agent trained on historical data may perform poorly when structure changes.

Mitigation strategies:

- Rolling retraining
- Regime-aware state features
- Conservative policy updates
- But complete stability is impossible.

3. Sparse and Delayed Rewards

In many trading strategies:

- Profits accumulate slowly
- Large moves occur infrequently
- Losses may be clustered

Reward signals can be sparse and delayed.

Example:

- Agent enters position.
- Market drifts sideways for days.
- Sudden move generates large reward or loss.

Credit assignment becomes difficult:

- Which earlier actions caused the outcome?

- High discount factors can help but increase variance.

4. Transaction Costs and Market Impact

Simulated RL environments often assume:

- Instant execution
- No slippage
- Fixed spreads

Real markets include:

- Spread variability
- Slippage
- Partial fills
- Market impact

If cost modeling is unrealistic, the agent will learn behavior that exploits simulation assumptions.

Common RL pathology:

- Overtrading because reward ignores cost
- Scalping small price moves that vanish after fees

Cost-aware reward design is mandatory.

5. Exploration Risk

RL requires exploration to discover better strategies.

In markets, exploration means:

- Taking suboptimal trades
- Incurring real losses

During live trading, exploration is costly.

Most RL research assumes exploration is safe. In trading, it is capital destructive.

Practical solution:

- Conduct exploration in historical simulation.
- Restrict exploration in live deployment.

However, limited live exploration reduces adaptability.

This creates a structural tension.

6. Sample Inefficiency

RL methods often require large numbers of episodes.

Financial data is limited.

Example:

- Daily data over 20 years = ~5,000 observations.
- Intraday data increases count but not independent information.

Compared to millions of training samples in gaming, financial RL operates with sparse data.

Overparameterized RL models overfit quickly.

7. Partial Observability

Markets are partially observable systems.

You do not observe:

- Full institutional order flow
- Hidden liquidity
- Private information
- Upcoming macro decisions

State representation is incomplete.

This violates the full Markov assumption.

Agents must approximate environment state using limited signals.

Poor state design severely limits learning quality.

8. Adversarial and Reflexive Environment

Markets are not static environments. Other participants:

- Learn
- Adapt
- Deploy AI systems
- Arbitrage predictable behavior

If your RL agent discovers a consistent edge, others may erode it.

This reflexivity makes long-term policy stability difficult.

The environment reacts to strategies.

9. Overfitting to Historical Simulation

RL agents often train in backtest environments.

Risks:

- Learning to exploit backtest artifacts
- Exploiting unrealistic liquidity
- Memorizing specific historical sequences

Without strict walk-forward validation, agents can show exceptional historical performance and fail immediately live.

Robust evaluation is harder in RL because behavior evolves during training.

10. Reward Design Fragility

Small changes in reward function can drastically alter behavior.

Example:

Reward = pnl

→ Aggressive leverage.

Reward = pnl − cost

→ Reduced turnover.

Reward = pnl − cost − drawdown_penalty

→ More conservative behavior.

Reward tuning can inadvertently become overfitting.

If reward is too complex, the agent optimizes a distorted objective.

11. Computational Complexity

RL training is computationally expensive.

- Multiple episodes
- Replay buffers
- Large neural networks

- Hyperparameter tuning

Financial institutions with significant infrastructure can manage this.

Individual traders may not justify cost relative to incremental performance gain.

12. Evaluation Difficulty

Supervised learning evaluates static predictions.

RL evaluates dynamic behavior.

Performance depends on:

- Policy stability
- Execution modeling
- Interaction effects

Walk-forward testing must simulate:

- Rolling retraining
- Cost changes
- Regime shifts

Evaluation complexity is significantly higher.

13. When RL Is Justified

Reinforcement learning is most appropriate when:

- Decision-making is sequential and path-dependent.
- Position sizing and risk control are dynamic.
- Portfolio allocation adapts continuously.
- Execution optimization is required.

Less appropriate when:

- Strategy is simple directional forecasting.
- Horizon is long and static.
- Signal is linear and stable.

In many cases, supervised learning plus rule-based risk control is sufficient.

Practical Risk Controls for RL Deployment

Before live deployment:

- Hard-code leverage limits.
- Enforce maximum drawdown cutoffs.
- Stress-test under increased transaction costs.
- Validate across multiple historical subperiods.
- Monitor rolling performance continuously.

RL agents should operate within strict guardrails.

Final Principle

Reinforcement learning promises adaptive, autonomous trading.

Markets respond with:

- Noise
- Regime shifts
- Cost friction
- Adversarial competition

RL in trading is not impossible.

It is simply harder than most other domains because the environment is:

- Unstable
- Noisy
- Competitive
- Capital-constrained

The success of RL systems in markets depends less on algorithm sophistication and more on:

- Conservative design
- Realistic simulation
- Strict risk control
- Continuous monitoring

In financial markets, intelligence without discipline is expensive.

Chapter 8: Agent Architectures and System Design

At some point, a notebook stops being enough. I've broken systems by adding "just one more component" more times than I'd like to admit. Good architecture isn't optional when agents run unattended.

This chapter discusses single-agent and multi-agent architectures, modular system design, and scalable decision pipelines.

8.1 Single-Agent vs Multi-Agent Trading Systems

As trading systems grow in complexity, one architectural question becomes unavoidable: Should one agent control everything, or should multiple agents specialize and coordinate?

This is not just a design preference. It affects:

- Stability
- Scalability
- Risk containment
- Debugging complexity
- Organizational structure of the system

Most production-grade systems are not purely single-agent or purely multi-agent. They are layered hybrids.

This section explains the trade-offs clearly and practically.

1. What Is a Single-Agent Trading System?

A single-agent system uses one decision-making entity to:

- Observe market state
- Generate signals
- Determine position size
- Execute trades
- Manage risk

Conceptually:

state = observe_market()

action = policy(state)

execute(action)

All logic flows through one policy.

Advantages of Single-Agent Systems

1. Simplicity

- Easier to implement
- Easier to train
- Easier to evaluate

Fewer moving parts mean fewer coordination failures.

2. Clear Objective Optimization

One reward function governs behavior.

This avoids conflicts between components.

Example:

reward = pnl - cost - risk_penalty

The agent directly optimizes portfolio-level performance.

3. Easier Attribution

If performance degrades, debugging is more straightforward.

You inspect:

- State representation
- Policy output
- Reward structure

No inter-agent blame shifting.

Limitations of Single-Agent Systems

1. Overloaded Decision Space

One agent may need to:

- Forecast signals
- Adjust risk
- Allocate capital
- Optimize execution

This creates a high-dimensional action space.

Learning becomes unstable.

2. Reduced Modularity

Changing one component (e.g., execution logic) may require retraining the entire system.

This slows iteration.

3. Scaling Challenges

In multi-asset portfolios, a single policy controlling dozens or hundreds of instruments becomes complex and data-hungry.

2. What Is a Multi-Agent Trading System?

A multi-agent system divides responsibilities across specialized agents.

Example architecture:

- Signal Agent
- Risk Agent
- Execution Agent
- Portfolio Allocation Agent

Each agent operates within a defined scope.

Conceptually:

signal = signal_agent(state)

position_size = risk_agent(signal, portfolio_state)

execution_agent(position_size)

Agents communicate through structured interfaces.

3. Types of Multi-Agent Structures

Horizontal Multi-Agent

Multiple agents trade independently on different assets.

Example:

- One agent per stock
- One agent per futures contract

Portfolio-level constraints overlay them.

This is common in systematic equity trading.

Vertical Multi-Agent

Agents operate at different decision layers:

- Strategy selection
- Signal generation
- Risk control
- Execution

Each layer focuses on a narrower task.

Competitive Multi-Agent

Agents compete for capital allocation.

Example:

weights = capital_allocator(strategy_outputs)

Each strategy proposes positions. Allocator distributes capital based on performance or risk-adjusted metrics.

4. Advantages of Multi-Agent Systems

1. Specialization

Each agent solves a simpler problem.

- Execution agent focuses only on minimizing slippage.
- Signal agent focuses on alpha generation.
- Risk agent focuses on exposure control.

Simpler learning tasks improve stability.

2. Modularity

Components can be replaced independently.

If execution degrades, retrain only execution agent.

Faster iteration cycle.

3. Scalability

Multi-asset expansion becomes easier.

Each asset-level agent operates independently while sharing higher-level constraints.

4. Risk Isolation

If one strategy fails, others continue operating.

Reduces systemic failure risk.

5. Challenges of Multi-Agent Systems

1. Coordination Complexity

Agents may conflict.

Example:

- Signal agent increases position.
- Risk agent reduces exposure simultaneously.

Coordination rules must be explicit.

2. Credit Assignment

If portfolio performance drops:

- Was it signal quality?
- Risk sizing?
- Execution slippage?

Debugging becomes multi-layered.

3. Emergent Instability

Interactions between agents can create unintended feedback loops.

Example:

- Risk agent reduces size during volatility spike.
- Execution agent increases urgency.
- Combined effect worsens slippage.

System-level simulation becomes essential.

6. Communication and Information Sharing

Agents must share structured information:

Example state exchange:

shared_state = {

"portfolio_exposure": total_exposure,

"current_volatility": market_vol,

"capital_available": capital

}

Poorly defined interfaces create inconsistency.

Clear boundaries are critical.

7. When to Use Single-Agent Systems

Appropriate when:

- Strategy scope is narrow.
- Asset universe is small.
- Decision process is tightly integrated.
- Research resources are limited.

Example:

- A single-asset reinforcement learning trader with continuous position sizing.

8. When to Use Multi-Agent Systems

Appropriate when:

- Trading multiple asset classes.
- Combining diverse strategies.
- Separating signal and execution logic.
- Scaling institutional-grade systems.

Example:

- Equity long/short strategy + macro overlay + execution optimizer.

9. Hybrid Approach (Most Practical)

Common production structure:

- Supervised model generates signals.
- Risk module applies position constraints.
- Execution module optimizes fills.
- Portfolio allocator balances across strategies.

Each component may use ML internally but is not fully autonomous.

This layered architecture improves robustness.

10. Risk Control in Multi-Agent Systems

Regardless of structure:

- Global risk limits must override local agent decisions.
- Capital constraints must be centralized.
- Emergency kill-switch must exist at system level.

Hard-coded example:

if portfolio_drawdown > max_allowed:

disable_all_agents()

System-level guardrails are mandatory.

Final Principle

Single-agent systems optimize coherence and simplicity.

Multi-agent systems optimize specialization and scalability.

As system complexity increases, single-agent architectures become harder to manage.

As modularity increases, coordination risk increases.

The correct choice depends on:

- Strategy breadth
- Asset universe size
- Infrastructure capability
- Organizational needs

In trading system design, architecture matters as much as model quality.

Poor architecture can destroy good signals.

Well-designed architecture can stabilize imperfect models.

8.2 Modular Agent Design and Decision Pipelines

As trading systems evolve, complexity grows naturally:

- More features
- More models
- More instruments
- More risk constraints
- More execution logic

Without modular design, complexity becomes fragility.

A modular agent architecture separates responsibilities into clearly defined components connected through structured interfaces. This improves:

- Stability
- Scalability
- Debugging
- Deployment reliability

In production systems, modularity is not optional. It is structural risk management.

1. What Is Modular Design in Trading Systems?

Modular design means:

- Each component performs one clearly defined function and communicates through explicit inputs and outputs.

Instead of:

action = giant_model(raw_data)

You build:

features = feature_module(raw_data)

signal = signal_model(features)

position = risk_module(signal, portfolio_state)

execution_module(position)

Each module can be developed, tested, and replaced independently.

2. Core Modules in a Trading Agent Pipeline

A practical modular trading system usually contains the following layers:

- Data Layer
- Feature Engineering Layer
- Signal Generation Layer
- Risk & Position Sizing Layer
- Portfolio Allocation Layer
- Execution Layer
- Monitoring Layer

Each module has a specific role.

3. Data Module

Responsibilities:

- Data ingestion
- Cleaning
- Timestamp alignment
- Normalization

Output:

- Structured state object

Example:

state = data_pipeline.get_state(current_time)

The data module must behave identically in:

- Backtesting
- Paper trading
- Live trading

Mismatch between research and production pipelines is a common failure point.

4. Feature Engineering Module

Transforms raw state into model-ready features.

features = feature_engineer.transform(state)

Responsibilities:

- Rolling calculations
- Regime indicators
- Volatility scaling
- Cross-asset relationships

Feature engineering should not depend on downstream modules.

This isolation prevents circular dependencies.

5. Signal Generation Module

Produces directional or probabilistic predictions.

signal = model.predict(features)

Examples:

- Probability of upward move
- Expected return
- Regime classification

Important:

Signal module should not directly manage capital.

Its job is prediction, not allocation.

Separation improves clarity and testing.

6. Risk and Position Sizing Module

Converts signal into position size.

position = risk_manager.allocate(signal, portfolio_state)

Responsibilities:

- Leverage control
- Volatility scaling
- Drawdown constraints

- Exposure limits

Example logic:

if volatility > threshold:

*position_size *= 0.5*

Risk module must enforce hard constraints independent of signal confidence.

Risk rules should not be learned. They should be deterministic.

7. Portfolio Allocation Module

When multiple strategies exist:

weights = allocator.allocate(strategy_outputs)

Responsibilities:

- Capital distribution
- Correlation control
- Risk budgeting
- Strategy weighting

This module prevents internal competition from destabilizing the portfolio.

8. Execution Module

Responsible for:

- Order type selection
- Slippage control
- Scheduling
- Market impact reduction

Example:

execution_engine.place_order(

symbol, quantity, order_type="limit"

)

Execution logic must be isolated from signal generation.

Otherwise, modeling assumptions about fill quality leak into prediction stage.

9. Monitoring and Logging Module

Often overlooked but critical.

Responsibilities:

- Performance tracking
- Risk exposure monitoring
- Latency monitoring
- Model drift detection

Example metrics:

- Rolling Sharpe
- Realized slippage
- Prediction accuracy decay

Without monitoring, modular design loses its advantage.

10. Decision Pipeline Flow

A typical real-time decision pipeline:

- Ingest new market data
- Update state
- Generate features
- Produce signal
- Apply risk constraints
- Determine target position
- Execute trades
- Log outcome

Simplified representation:

state = data_module.update()

features = feature_module.transform(state)

signal = signal_module.predict(features)

position = risk_module.compute(signal, portfolio_state)

execution_module.execute(position)

monitor_module.log()

Each step is independently testable.

11. Benefits of Modular Pipelines

1. Easier Debugging

If performance drops:

- Check signal quality
- Check slippage changes
- Check risk adjustment behavior

Isolation accelerates root-cause analysis.

2. Safer Iteration

You can improve one module without rewriting the entire system.

Example:

- Replace linear model with CNN without modifying execution logic.

3. Parallel Development

Different teams can work on:

- Data
- Modeling
- Execution
- Risk

Without interfering with each other's code.

4. Production Reliability

Failure in one module can trigger controlled fallback.

Example:

If model fails:

use_backup_signal()

Fail-safe mechanisms are easier in modular systems.

12. Anti-Patterns to Avoid

- Mixing signal and risk logic inside same model.
- Allowing execution feedback to alter signal directly.
- Sharing mutable state across modules without clear interface.
- Building monolithic code that cannot be unit tested.

Monolithic systems are hard to audit and harder to scale.

13. Designing Clean Interfaces

Each module should define:

- Input schema
- Output schema
- Constraints

Example:

Signal module:

Input:

- Feature vector

Output:

- Float between -1 and 1

Risk module:

Input:

- Signal
- Portfolio state

Output:

- Target position

Clear contracts prevent unintended coupling.

14. Testing Each Module Independently

Unit test examples:

- Feature values at specific timestamps
- Risk module enforcing max exposure
- Execution module simulating partial fills

Robust trading systems treat software engineering discipline as part of alpha preservation.

Final Principle

Modular design separates:

- Prediction
- Risk control
- Capital allocation
- Execution

Each layer has different objectives.

When these concerns are entangled, systems become fragile and opaque.

When they are modular, systems become:

- Scalable
- Testable
- Replaceable
- Safer to operate

In autonomous trading systems, architecture is not infrastructure.

It is part of risk management.

8.3 Communication and Coordination Between Agents

Once you introduce multiple agents into a trading system, the core challenge is no longer just decision-making. It becomes coordination.

Without clear communication rules, multi-agent systems drift into:

- Conflicting positions
- Capital over-allocation
- Redundant trades
- Hidden systemic risk

In financial systems, poor coordination does not reduce performance slightly. It amplifies instability.

This section focuses on:

- Communication architecture
- Coordination strategies
- Conflict resolution mechanisms
- System-level stability

1. Why Coordination Matters

Consider three agents:

- Momentum agent
- Mean-reversion agent
- Volatility breakout agent

Without coordination:

- Two agents go long
- One goes short
- Portfolio exposure oscillates
- Execution costs increase

Even worse, agents may unknowingly increase leverage beyond intended limits.

Coordination ensures the portfolio behaves as a coherent system rather than independent actors sharing capital.

2. Communication Architecture

Communication between agents must be structured and explicit.

Two primary models:

- Centralized coordination
- Decentralized communication

2.1 Centralized Coordination

A central controller aggregates outputs from all agents.

Example:

signals = {

"momentum": 0.8,

"mean_reversion": -0.4,

"breakout": 0.3

}

final_position = allocator.combine(signals)

The central allocator:

- Weights signals
- Applies capital constraints
- Resolves conflicts

Advantages:

- Clear global control
- Easier risk enforcement
- Simpler debugging

Most institutional systems use centralized portfolio control.

2.2 Decentralized Communication

Agents share state information directly with each other.

Example shared state:

shared_state = {

"portfolio_exposure": total_exposure,

"volatility_regime": regime,

"available_capital": capital

EACH AGENT ADJUSTS behavior based on shared variables.

Advantages:

- More flexible
- Potentially adaptive
- Lower central bottleneck

Risks:

- Emergent instability
- Harder to debug
- Coordination loops

Decentralized systems require strict communication protocols.

3. Communication Methods

3.1 Message Passing

Agents send structured messages:

message = {

"agent_id": "momentum",

"proposed_position": 1000,

"confidence": 0.75

}

Messages are processed by a coordination layer.

Clear message schema prevents ambiguity.

3.2 Shared Memory (State Object)

All agents read from and write to a shared portfolio state.

Example:

```
portfolio_state.update({
"exposure": new_exposure
})
```

Must implement:

- Locking mechanisms
- Update order rules
- Consistency checks

Otherwise, race conditions occur.

3.3 Hierarchical Communication

Higher-level agent oversees lower-level agents.

Structure:

- Strategy agents generate signals
- Risk supervisor modifies limits
- Execution supervisor schedules orders

This creates controlled flow of authority.

4. Coordination Strategies

4.1 Weighted Aggregation

Combine signals linearly:

```
final_signal = (
w1 * signal_1 +
w2 * signal_2 +
w3 * signal_3
)
```

Weights may be:

- Fixed
- Performance-based

- Volatility-adjusted

Simple and stable approach.

4.2 Risk Budgeting

Allocate capital according to risk contribution.

Example:

target_weight = risk_budget / strategy_volatility

Ensures one agent does not dominate risk exposure.

4.3 Voting Mechanism

Agents vote on direction.

Example:

- **Majority long** → go long
- **Majority short** → go short

Simple but may discard magnitude information.

4.4 Competitive Capital Allocation

Each agent proposes expected return and risk.

Allocator solves optimization:

- Maximize portfolio expected return subject to risk constraints.
- More advanced but computationally heavier.

5. Conflict Resolution

Conflicts are inevitable.

Example conflict:

- Agent A wants +100 units
- Agent B wants -100 units

Resolution methods:

- Netting (sum signals)
- Priority hierarchy (one agent overrides)
- Confidence-weighted aggregation

- Regime-based dominance

Example:

if regime == "trending":

weight_momentum = 0.7

weight_mean_reversion = 0.3

Explicit conflict rules reduce instability.

6. Preventing Coordination Failures

Hard Global Constraints

Regardless of agent outputs:

if total_exposure > max_allowed:

scale_down_positions()

System-level risk limits override individual decisions.

Exposure Tracking

Track:

- Net exposure
- Gross exposure
- Sector exposure
- Asset concentration

Agents must be aware of shared constraints.

Order Synchronization

Multiple agents placing orders simultaneously increases slippage.

Centralized execution batching reduces market impact.

7. Avoiding Feedback Loops

Uncontrolled coordination can create feedback cycles.

Example:

- Agent A reduces exposure due to volatility.
- This increases portfolio drawdown.

- Risk module tightens limits further.
- Agents reduce positions excessively.

Overreaction can destabilize the system.

Mitigation:

- Smoothing adjustments
- Gradual scaling
- Constraint damping

Example:

*position = previous_position * 0.9 + new_signal * 0.1*

This reduces abrupt shifts.

8. Monitoring Multi-Agent Health

Track:

- Individual agent performance
- Correlation between agents
- Capital allocation shifts
- Conflict frequency

If two agents are highly correlated, diversification benefit is low.

If one agent consistently dominates capital, system balance may degrade.

9. Practical Design Principles

- Keep communication structured and minimal.
- Centralize risk constraints.
- Separate signal generation from allocation decisions.
- Log inter-agent decisions for auditability.
- Test stress scenarios where agents disagree sharply.

Complex coordination requires stronger monitoring.

Final Principle

Multi-agent systems increase flexibility and specialization.

They also increase coordination risk.

Communication defines:

- Who decides
- Who adapts
- Who overrides

Without explicit coordination rules, agents behave independently and destabilize the portfolio.

With structured communication and centralized risk control, multi-agent systems become scalable, resilient architectures for complex trading environments.

In autonomous trading systems, coordination is not an optimization problem.

It is a stability problem.

Chapter 9: Strategy Design and Signal Generation

Alpha is not something you stumble into accidentally. Every signal has an assumption hiding inside it, and markets love breaking assumptions. I learned that combining weak signals intelligently beats chasing mythical perfect ones.

This chapter focuses on systematic strategy design, signal validation, ensemble methods, and regime-aware modeling.

9.1 Alpha Discovery and Hypothesis Testing

Alpha is not discovered by accident. It is discovered by forming a hypothesis about market behavior and testing it under realistic conditions.

Most failed strategies are not bad ideas. They are poorly tested ideas.

In systematic trading, alpha discovery should follow a disciplined process:

- Define an economic hypothesis
- Translate it into measurable signals
- Test statistically
- Validate economically
- Stress test robustness

Without this structure, you are data mining.

1. What Is Alpha?

Alpha is excess return relative to a benchmark after adjusting for risk and costs.

More precisely:

- Alpha is a persistent, tradable statistical edge that survives transaction costs and regime variation.

Key requirements:

- Repeatable
- Statistically significant
- Economically meaningful
- Deployable at scale

High in-sample performance is not alpha.

2. Starting with an Economic Hypothesis

Alpha begins with a behavioral or structural idea.

Examples:

- Momentum persists due to underreaction.

- Mean reversion occurs due to liquidity imbalances.
- Volatility clustering creates regime persistence.
- Earnings surprises cause delayed price adjustment.

Weak starting point:

- *"I ran 500 indicators and found something that works."*

Strong starting point:

- *"I believe volatility expansion leads to short-term continuation because liquidity providers widen spreads."*

Hypothesis first. Data second.

3. Translating Hypothesis into a Signal

Convert economic intuition into measurable variables.

Example: Momentum hypothesis.

Signal construction:

momentum = price / price.shift(20) - 1

signal = momentum.shift(1)

EXAMPLE: MEAN REVERSION hypothesis.

rolling_mean = price.rolling(50).mean().shift(1)

rolling_std = price.rolling(50).std().shift(1)

z_score = (price - rolling_mean) / rolling_std

signal = -z_score

Signal must be:

- Observable in real time
- Free from look-ahead bias
- Economically interpretable

4. Statistical Hypothesis Testing

Once signal is defined, test statistical validity.

4.1 Null Hypothesis

Null hypothesis:

- The signal has no predictive power.

Test correlation between signal and future returns:

corr = np.corrcoef(signal, future_return)[0, 1]

Evaluate:

- t-statistic
- P-value

However, statistical significance alone is insufficient.

Large datasets can make small, meaningless effects appear significant.

4.2 Information Coefficient (IC)

Common metric in alpha research:

ic = np.corrcoef(signal, future_return)[0, 1]

Track:

- Average IC
- IC stability over time

A signal with IC of 0.03 may be meaningful in cross-sectional trading.

Consistency matters more than magnitude.

5. Economic Significance Testing

Statistical significance does not guarantee tradability.

Test strategy performance:

*strategy_return = signal * future_return*

Evaluate:

- Sharpe ratio
- Drawdown
- Turnover
- Net return after costs

If expected edge per trade is smaller than transaction cost, reject.

6. Cross-Validation and Walk-Forward Testing

Divide data into sequential windows:

- Train
- Validate
- Slide forward

Repeat across multiple periods.

Performance must be:

- Stable across time
- Not concentrated in one regime
- Not driven by a single outlier period

If alpha disappears in out-of-sample testing, it was likely noise.

7. Multiple Testing Problem

Testing many ideas increases probability of false discoveries.

If you test 100 independent signals, some will appear significant by chance.

Mitigation:

- Limit hypothesis count
- Adjust for multiple comparisons
- Keep research log
- Separate research and validation datasets

Avoid tuning signal thresholds excessively.

Every additional parameter increases overfitting risk.

8. Robustness Testing

After initial validation, stress the signal.

Test variations:

- Different lookback windows
- Different holding periods
- Different transaction cost assumptions

- Different subperiods

Example:

for lookback in [10, 20, 30, 40]:

test_signal(lookback)

If signal only works at exactly 23-day lookback but fails at 20 or 25, it is fragile.

Robust signals show gradual performance decay when parameters shift slightly.

9. Capacity and Scalability

A signal that works on small size may fail at scale.

Evaluate:

- Liquidity constraints
- Slippage sensitivity

Market impact

Simulate larger position sizes and measure performance degradation.

Alpha that disappears under realistic volume assumptions is not deployable.

10. Regime Sensitivity

Test performance across:

- Bull markets
- Bear markets
- High volatility regimes
- Low volatility regimes

If alpha works only in one regime, treat it as conditional strategy.

Regime-aware combination may improve stability.

11. Decay Monitoring

After deployment, monitor signal degradation.

Track rolling performance:

*rolling_sharpe = strategy_return.rolling(252).mean() / *

strategy_return.rolling(252).std()

If rolling IC declines persistently, alpha may be decaying.

Markets adapt. Alpha is rarely permanent.

12. Research Discipline Framework

For each candidate alpha:

- Define economic rationale.
- Construct measurable signal.
- Test statistical significance.
- Validate economic performance.
- Perform walk-forward testing.
- Stress-test robustness.
- Evaluate scalability.
- Document assumptions.

If any step fails, refine or discard.

Discarding weak signals is part of professional research.

Final Principle

Alpha discovery is not indicator hunting.

It is structured hypothesis testing under uncertainty.

A valid alpha:

- Has economic reasoning.
- Shows statistical consistency.
- Survives cost assumptions.
- Remains stable across time.
- Scales under realistic liquidity constraints.

The objective is not to find the highest historical return.

It is to identify durable edges that survive contact with real markets.

In systematic trading, disciplined rejection is as important as discovery.

9.2 Combining Multiple Signals and Models

No single signal dominates markets consistently. Momentum fails in range-bound markets. Mean reversion collapses during breakouts. Volatility signals decay when conditions normalize.

Durable performance usually comes from combining multiple weak signals into a structured system.

The objective of signal combination is not complexity. It is stability.

This section focuses on:

- Why combining signals improves robustness
- Methods for signal aggregation
- Model ensembles
- Risk-aware combination techniques
- Practical validation

1. Why Combine Signals?

Individual signals often have:

- Low predictive power
- Regime sensitivity
- High variance

Combining signals can:

- Reduce variance
- Smooth equity curves
- Improve risk-adjusted returns
- Reduce dependency on a single market condition

If signals are imperfect but partially independent, aggregation improves stability.

This is diversification applied to alpha.

2. Basic Linear Combination

The simplest approach:

```
combined_signal = (
w1 * signal_1 +
w2 * signal_2 +
w3 * signal_3
)
```

Weights may be:

- Equal
- Performance-based
- Volatility-adjusted
- Equal weighting is often a strong baseline.

Over-optimizing weights on historical data increases overfitting risk.

3. Normalization Before Combination

Signals must be normalized before aggregation.

Example using z-score normalization:

```
signal_z = (signal - signal.rolling(100).mean().shift(1)) / \
signal.rolling(100).std().shift(1)
```

Without normalization:

- Large-scale signals dominate
- Interpretation becomes inconsistent

Ensure signals are comparable in magnitude and direction.

4. Weighted Combination Based on Performance

Weights can adapt based on rolling performance.

Example:

```
rolling_sharpe_1 = compute_sharpe(signal_1_returns)
rolling_sharpe_2 = compute_sharpe(signal_2_returns)
total = abs(rolling_sharpe_1) + abs(rolling_sharpe_2)
w1 = abs(rolling_sharpe_1) / total
```

w2 = abs(rolling_sharpe_2) / total

This allows capital to shift toward better-performing signals.

Risk:

- Overreacting to short-term noise
- Increasing turnover

Smoothing is recommended.

5. Correlation-Aware Combination

If two signals are highly correlated, combining them provides limited diversification.

Measure correlation:

corr = np.corrcoef(signal_1, signal_2)[0, 1]

If correlation is high, reduce combined weight.

Risk-aware weighting example:

- Lower weight for signals with high pairwise correlation
- Favor uncorrelated signals

This reduces concentrated exposure.

6. Ensemble Models

Instead of combining signals manually, combine model outputs.

Example:

- Linear regression model
- Random forest model
- Neural network model

Ensemble prediction:

ensemble_pred = (

*0.4 * linear_pred +*

*0.3 * tree_pred +*

*0.3 * nn_pred*

)

Ensembles often outperform individual models because:

- Different models capture different patterns
- Errors are partially uncorrelated

However, ensure models are genuinely diverse.

Using three similar gradient boosting models provides limited benefit.

7. Stacking (Meta-Modeling)

Advanced ensemble method:

- Train base models
- Use their predictions as features
- Train a meta-model

Example:

meta_features = np.column_stack([pred_1, pred_2, pred_3])

meta_model.fit(meta_features, target)

This allows learning nonlinear combinations.

Risk:

- Increased overfitting
- Requires strict walk-forward validation

Use only when dataset size supports complexity.

8. Regime-Based Signal Switching

Instead of blending signals continuously, switch based on detected regime.

Example:

if regime == "trending":

final_signal = momentum_signal

elif regime == "range":

final_signal = mean_reversion_signal

This conditional structure can improve performance if regime detection is reliable.

Risk:

- Incorrect regime classification
- Increased model complexity

Often better to weight signals rather than hard-switch.

9. Risk-Based Position Aggregation

Signal combination must integrate with risk management.

After combining signals:

position = risk_scaler(combined_signal)

Risk scaler may:

- Volatility scale
- Enforce max exposure
- Cap concentration

Even strong signals must respect portfolio constraints.

10. Avoiding Over-Optimization

Common mistake:

- Optimizing signal weights to maximize historical Sharpe.

This often leads to unstable allocations.

Mitigation:

- Use coarse weight grids
- Apply regularization
- Test across subperiods
- Penalize high turnover

If optimal weight shifts dramatically across periods, system is unstable.

11. Turnover and Cost Consideration

Combining signals may increase trade frequency.

Monitor:

turnover = abs(position.diff()).sum()

If combination improves gross Sharpe but increases turnover significantly, net performance may degrade.

Always evaluate after transaction costs.

12. Practical Validation Checklist

Before deploying combined strategy:

- Signals normalized consistently.
- Correlation between signals evaluated.
- Weight stability tested across time.
- Performance stable in walk-forward testing.
- Transaction costs included.
- No single signal dominates risk exposure.

If removing one signal collapses performance, diversification is weak.

Final Principle

Combining signals is about diversification of edge.

Weak but independent signals can produce strong, stable performance when structured correctly.

However:

- Poor weighting introduces overfitting.
- Ignoring correlation concentrates risk.
- Excessive complexity increases fragility.

The objective is not to maximize historical Sharpe.

It is to construct a portfolio of signals that:

- Complement each other
- Survive regime shifts
- Remain stable under cost pressure

In systematic trading, robustness comes not from one brilliant idea, but from disciplined aggregation of multiple imperfect ones.

9.3 Regime-Aware and Adaptive Strategies

Markets do not behave consistently across time. Strategies that work in low-volatility trending markets often fail during high-volatility reversals. Static systems assume stability. Markets rarely provide it.

Regime-aware and adaptive strategies explicitly recognize that:

- Market structure shifts
- Volatility changes
- Correlations evolve
- Liquidity conditions fluctuate

Instead of forcing one model to perform in all conditions, regime-aware systems adjust behavior based on the environment.

This section focuses on practical implementation of adaptive strategies.

1. What Is a Market Regime?

A regime is a persistent state of market behavior characterized by:

- Volatility level
- Trend strength
- Correlation structure
- Liquidity conditions

Examples:

- High-volatility risk-off regime
- Low-volatility mean-reverting regime
- Strong trending regime
- Crisis regime

Regimes are not labeled by the market. They must be inferred from data.

2. Detecting Regimes

Regime detection methods were introduced earlier. In practice, common approaches include:

- Volatility thresholds

- Trend indicators
- Clustering models
- Hidden Markov Models

Example simple volatility regime:

vol_short = returns.rolling(20).std().shift(1)

vol_long = returns.rolling(100).std().shift(1)

*regime = (vol_short > 1.5 * vol_long).astype(int)*

- **Regime = 1** → High volatility
- **Regime = 0** → Normal volatility

Keep detection simple. Complex regime models often overfit.

3. Strategy Switching

One straightforward adaptation method is conditional strategy activation.

Example:

if regime == 1: # High volatility

signal = breakout_strategy(features)

else:

signal = mean_reversion_strategy(features)

Advantages:

- Clear separation of logic
- Intuitive design
- Easy debugging

Risks:

- Regime misclassification
- Over-sensitivity to switching
- Increased turnover

Smoothing regime transitions can reduce instability.

4. Regime-Based Weight Adjustment

Instead of switching fully, adjust weights dynamically.

Example:

if regime == 1:

w_momentum = 0.7

w_mean_rev = 0.3

else:

w_momentum = 0.3

w_mean_rev = 0.7

*combined_signal = w_momentum * momentum + w_mean_rev * mean_reversion*

This reduces abrupt changes.

Gradual weighting often improves robustness.

5. Volatility Scaling

Volatility is one of the most stable regime indicators.

Dynamic position sizing:

target_vol = 0.15

current_vol = returns.rolling(20).std().shift(1)

position_size = target_vol / (current_vol + 1e-6)

When volatility increases, position size decreases.

Volatility scaling improves drawdown control and stabilizes returns across regimes.

6. Adaptive Parameter Adjustment

Instead of changing strategies, adjust parameters.

Example:

Shorter lookback in high volatility:

if regime == 1:

lookback = 10

else:

lookback = 30

Or adaptive threshold:

*threshold = k * current_vol*

This maintains relative sensitivity across environments.

However, avoid excessive parameter flexibility. Too many adaptive knobs introduce overfitting.

7. Reinforcement Learning for Adaptation

RL agents can incorporate regime information into state representation.

Example state:

state = {

"features": feature_vector,

"vol_regime": regime,

"drawdown": current_drawdown

}

The agent learns behavior conditional on regime.

Caution:

- RL adds complexity. If regime detection already works with simpler rules, do not escalate unnecessarily.

8. Regime-Specific Risk Control

Adaptation should apply to risk as well as signal generation.

Examples:

- Reduce leverage in high-volatility regime.
- Tighten stop-loss during crisis.
- Increase diversification when correlations rise.

Example:

if regime == "crisis":

max_leverage = 0.5

else:

max_leverage = 1.0

Risk adaptation often contributes more stability than signal adaptation.

9. Avoiding Regime Overfitting

Common mistake:

- Creating too many regimes.

If you define:

- Bull market
- Bear market
- Sideways
- High volatility
- Low volatility
- Recovery phase
- Panic phase

You risk fitting noise.

Keep regime classification coarse and stable.

Test:

- Regime persistence
- Transition frequency
- Performance within each regime

If regime changes daily, detection is capturing noise.

10. Walk-Forward Validation

Regime-aware strategies must be validated carefully.

For each walk-forward period:

- Detect regime using only past data.
- Apply strategy logic.
- Evaluate performance.

Do not compute regime labels using full dataset before testing.

Regime detection itself must be part of training pipeline.

11. Monitoring Regime Drift

Markets may evolve structurally.

Track:

- Distribution of volatility
- Average correlation
- Spread behavior

If regime detection patterns shift significantly, recalibration may be required.

Avoid constant recalibration. Use scheduled updates.

12. Practical Design Guidelines

- Start with volatility-based adaptation.
- Use simple regime definitions.
- Prefer weight adjustment over hard switching.
- Enforce consistent risk constraints.
- Validate across multiple historical regimes.

Adaptive systems must improve stability—not simply increase complexity.

Final Principle

Static strategies assume markets are stable.

Regime-aware strategies assume markets change.

The objective is not to predict regime perfectly.

It is to reduce exposure when environment becomes unfavorable and increase allocation when conditions align with strategy strengths.

Adaptation should enhance robustness, not introduce instability.

In systematic trading, the most effective adaptation often occurs in risk management—not in signal generation.

Durability comes from flexibility under constraint.

Chapter 10: Risk Management and Position Sizing

This chapter exists because survival matters more than returns. I've seen brilliant strategies destroyed by poor risk control. The market doesn't reward bravery—it rewards staying in the game.

This chapter covers risk metrics, dynamic position sizing, drawdown control, and portfolio-level risk management techniques.

10.1 Risk Metrics: Volatility, Drawdown, and Tail Risk

Return attracts attention. Risk determines survival.

In systematic trading, most strategies fail not because they lack return, but because they misjudge risk. Risk must be measured continuously and integrated directly into decision-making.

This section focuses on three core categories of risk metrics:

- Volatility
- Drawdown
- Tail risk

Each captures a different dimension of uncertainty.

1. Volatility

Volatility measures variability of returns. It is the most widely used risk proxy.

1.1 Realized Volatility

Rolling standard deviation of returns:

volatility = returns.rolling(20).std()

Annualized volatility:

*annual_vol = volatility * np.sqrt(252)*

Volatility reflects dispersion but not direction.

High volatility implies larger expected price swings, both positive and negative.

1.2 Volatility as Position Scaling Tool

Volatility is often used to standardize risk exposure.

Example:

target_vol = 0.15

position_size = target_vol / (annual_vol + 1e-6)

When volatility increases, exposure decreases.

This stabilizes risk across regimes.

Volatility scaling is one of the most effective and simple risk controls in systematic trading.

1.3 Limitations of Volatility

Volatility assumes symmetric risk.

It does not distinguish between:

- Large gains
- Large losses

It also assumes distributional stability, which financial returns rarely exhibit.

Therefore, volatility alone is insufficient.

2. Drawdown

Drawdown measures peak-to-trough decline in portfolio value.

It reflects capital erosion and psychological stress.

2.1 Calculating Drawdown

cumulative = (1 + returns).cumprod()

rolling_max = cumulative.cummax()

drawdown = cumulative / rolling_max - 1

max_drawdown = drawdown.min()

Maximum drawdown (MDD) captures the worst historical loss from peak.

2.2 Why Drawdown Matters

Drawdown answers a practical question:

- How much capital can this strategy lose before recovering?

High drawdown:

- Reduces investor confidence
- Triggers redemptions
- May breach risk mandates

Two strategies with identical Sharpe ratios can have very different drawdown profiles.

2.3 Drawdown Duration

Depth is only part of the story.

Measure duration:

```
drawdown_duration = (drawdown < 0).astype(int).groupby(
(drawdown == 0).cumsum()
).sum().max()
```

Long recovery periods can be more damaging than deep but short drawdowns.

3. Tail Risk

Tail risk measures probability and magnitude of extreme losses.

Financial return distributions often exhibit:

- Fat tails
- Skewness
- Extreme events

Volatility does not capture this adequately.

3.1 Value at Risk (VaR)

VaR estimates potential loss at a confidence level.

Example 95% VaR:

```
var_95 = np.percentile(returns, 5)
```

Interpretation:

- With 95% confidence, loss should not exceed this value over specified horizon.

Limitations:

- Does not measure magnitude beyond threshold
- Assumes stable distribution

3.2 Conditional Value at Risk (CVaR)

Also called Expected Shortfall.

Measures average loss beyond VaR.

```
cvar_95 = returns[returns <= var_95].mean()
```

CVaR captures severity of tail events more effectively.

For tail-sensitive strategies, CVaR is often more informative than volatility.

3.3 Skewness and Kurtosis

Higher-order statistics help understand distribution shape.

skew = returns.skew()

kurt = returns.kurtosis()

Negative skewness implies higher likelihood of extreme losses.

High kurtosis implies fat tails.

Strategies with attractive Sharpe but negative skew are often vulnerable to sudden crashes.

4. Integrating Risk Metrics into Trading Systems

Risk metrics should not be passive reports. They should drive action.

4.1 Volatility-Based Risk Control

if annual_vol > vol_threshold:

reduce_position_size()

4.2 Drawdown-Based Stop Mechanism

if current_drawdown < -0.15:

reduce_leverage()

4.3 Tail Risk Guardrails

Stress-test using historical worst periods.

Example:

- Simulate 2008 conditions
- Simulate 2020 volatility spike

If strategy collapses under realistic tail scenarios, risk exposure must be reduced.

5. Trade-Off Between Return and Risk

Higher return strategies often:

- Exhibit higher volatility
- Have deeper drawdowns
- Show worse tail behavior

Risk-adjusted metrics like Sharpe or Calmar incorporate both return and risk.

Example Calmar ratio:

calmar = annual_return / abs(max_drawdown)

Risk-aware strategy design prioritizes stable risk-adjusted return over peak raw return.

6. Risk Across Multiple Horizons

Risk behaves differently across timescales.

Short-term volatility may spike without long-term trend change.

Monitor:

- Intraday volatility
- Daily volatility
- Rolling monthly volatility

Multi-horizon monitoring improves stability.

7. Common Risk Measurement Mistakes

- Using only volatility as risk metric.
- Ignoring tail risk in backtests.
- Measuring risk without transaction costs.
- Failing to update rolling risk metrics in live systems.
- Assuming historical worst case is sufficient.

Markets evolve. Risk metrics must adapt.

Practical Risk Monitoring Checklist

Before deploying a strategy:

- Calculate rolling volatility.
- Measure maximum drawdown and duration.
- Estimate VaR and CVaR.
- Analyze skewness and kurtosis.
- Stress-test extreme historical periods.
- Integrate risk limits into position sizing logic.

Risk management must be proactive, not reactive.

Final Principle

- Volatility measures variability.
- Drawdown measures capital erosion.
- Tail risk measures extreme vulnerability.

A strategy with strong returns but unmanaged tail risk is fragile.

Long-term survival in trading depends less on maximizing returns and more on controlling risk across all dimensions.

In systematic systems, risk metrics are not reporting tools.

They are control inputs that protect capital and ensure durability.

10.2 Dynamic Position Sizing and Capital Allocation

Signal quality determines direction. Position sizing determines outcome.

Two strategies with identical entry signals can produce dramatically different results depending on how capital is allocated. Most trading systems fail not because signals are wrong, but because exposure is poorly managed.

Dynamic position sizing adjusts capital allocation based on:

- Signal strength
- Volatility
- Portfolio exposure
- Drawdown
- Market regime

The objective is capital preservation with scalable upside.

1. Fixed Position Sizing (Baseline)

Simplest approach:

$position = signal * fixed\_size$

Example:

- Always trade 1 contract
- Always allocate 2% of capital

Advantages:

- Simple
- Easy to evaluate

Limitations:

- Ignores volatility changes
- Ignores portfolio interaction
- Ignores drawdown state

Fixed sizing is rarely optimal in adaptive markets.

2. Volatility-Adjusted Position Sizing

One of the most effective dynamic methods.

Principle:

- Risk per trade should remain constant even when volatility changes.

Example:

target_vol = 0.15

current_vol = returns.rolling(20).std().shift(1)

position_size = target_vol / (current_vol + 1e-6)

When volatility increases:

- Position size decreases
- When volatility decreases:
- Position size increases

This stabilizes portfolio risk across regimes.

3. Risk-Based Position Sizing

Define maximum acceptable loss per trade.

Example:

Risk 1% of capital per trade.

*risk_per_trade = 0.01 * capital*

stop_distance = abs(entry_price - stop_price)

position_size = risk_per_trade / stop_distance

This ensures consistent downside exposure.

Widely used in discretionary and systematic strategies.

4. Kelly Criterion (Capital Growth Maximization)

Kelly fraction:

$$f^* = \frac{p \cdot b - (1 - p)}{b}$$

Where:

- p = probability of win
- b = win/loss ratio

In practice, full Kelly is too aggressive.

Use fractional Kelly:

*position_size = kelly_fraction * 0.5*

Kelly maximizes long-term growth but increases drawdown volatility.

Rarely used at full strength in institutional systems.

5. Signal-Confidence Scaling

If model outputs probabilities:

proba = model.predict_proba(features)[1]

*position_size = 2 * (proba - 0.5)*

Higher confidence → larger allocation.

Requires calibrated probabilities.

Poor calibration leads to unstable exposure.

6. Drawdown-Based Scaling

When portfolio drawdown increases, reduce exposure.

Example:

if current_drawdown < -0.1:

leverage = 0.5

else:

leverage = 1.0

This reduces capital erosion during adverse periods.

Drawdown-based scaling improves survivability.

7. Portfolio-Level Capital Allocation

When multiple strategies exist, capital must be allocated across them.

Methods include:

- Equal weighting
- Risk parity
- Performance-based weighting
- Optimization-based allocation

7.1 Equal Weighting

Simple and surprisingly effective:

weight = 1 / number_of_strategies

Avoids overfitting allocation weights.

7.2 Risk Parity Allocation

Allocate capital based on risk contribution.

Example:

weight_i = 1 / volatility_i

normalized_weight = weight_i / sum(weights)

This equalizes volatility contribution across strategies.

Reduces dominance of high-volatility systems.

7.3 Performance-Based Allocation

Increase weight of better-performing strategies:

weight_i = rolling_sharpe_i

Must smooth to avoid overreaction.

Overweighting recent winners increases regime sensitivity.

7.4 Mean-Variance Optimization

Maximize expected return subject to risk constraint.

Requires:

- Expected return estimates
- Covariance matrix

Optimization example (conceptual):

$$\max_{w} \; w^T \mu - \lambda w^T \Sigma w$$

Powerful but sensitive to estimation error.

Often unstable in practice without regularization.

8. Correlation Awareness

Position sizing must consider cross-strategy correlation.

Two strategies both long equity index during crisis do not diversify risk.

Measure rolling correlation:

corr_matrix = returns_df.corr()

High correlation → reduce combined exposure.

Diversification reduces drawdown.

9. Leverage Management

Total exposure must respect leverage limits.

Example:

if gross_exposure > max_leverage:

scale_positions()

Gross and net exposure should both be monitored.

Leverage magnifies both alpha and error.

10. Dynamic Capital Allocation in Reinforcement Learning

In RL systems, position size may be continuous output:

action = policy(state)

*position = action * max_position*

Hard risk constraints must override learned behavior.

Never allow RL agent to self-regulate leverage without strict bounds.

11. Transaction Cost Impact on Sizing

Higher position adjustments increase turnover.

Monitor:

turnover = abs(position.diff()).sum()

If dynamic sizing improves gross Sharpe but increases turnover significantly, net performance may decline.

Always evaluate after costs.

12. Stress Testing Position Rules

Before deployment:

- Simulate volatility spike.
- Simulate correlation spike.
- Simulate drawdown period.

Increase transaction cost assumption.

Position sizing logic must remain stable.

Overly reactive sizing increases instability.

Practical Design Principles

- Start with volatility scaling.
- Add drawdown controls.
- Limit leverage explicitly.
- Avoid over-optimized allocation weights.

Test allocation stability across regimes.

Complex allocation methods should outperform simple equal weighting consistently before adoption.

Final Principle

Signal determines direction.

Position sizing determines survival and growth.

Dynamic capital allocation transforms weak but stable signals into robust portfolios.

Poor position sizing can destroy strong signals.

In systematic trading, risk-adjusted capital allocation is not a secondary layer.

It is the mechanism that converts alpha into durable performance.

10.3 Portfolio-Level Risk Control

Individual strategy risk management is not enough.

A portfolio can appear diversified at the strategy level while being highly concentrated at the risk level. True portfolio-level risk control looks beyond individual trades and focuses on:

- Total exposure
- Correlation structure
- Concentration risk
- Systemic vulnerability

The objective is to control aggregate risk, not just trade-level losses.

1. Net and Gross Exposure

The simplest portfolio-level metrics are:

- **Net exposure:** directional bias
- **Gross exposure**: total leverage

Net Exposure

$$\text{Net Exposure} = \sum w_i$$

Example:

net_exposure = positions.sum()

- **Positive** → net long
- **Negative** → net short

High net exposure increases directional risk.

Gross Exposure

$$\text{Gross Exposure} = \sum |w_i|$$

Example:

gross_exposure = abs(positions).sum()

Gross exposure measures total leverage.

Even if net exposure is zero, high gross exposure implies high risk.

Portfolio-level limits should cap both.

2. Concentration Risk

Large positions in a single asset or sector increase fragility.

Monitor:

- Maximum single-asset weight
- Sector exposure
- Asset-class exposure

Example constraint:

if abs(weight_i) > max_asset_weight:

weight_i = max_asset_weight

Diversification must be enforced systematically.

3. Correlation Risk

Diversification fails when correlations rise.

During stress events, assets often move together.

Monitor rolling correlation matrix:

corr_matrix = returns_df.rolling(60).corr()

High average pairwise correlation increases systemic risk.

If correlation spikes:

- Reduce leverage
- Increase diversification
- Tighten risk limits

Ignoring correlation clustering leads to unexpected drawdowns.

4. Portfolio Volatility

Portfolio-level volatility is more informative than individual asset volatility.

$$\sigma_p = \sqrt{w^T \Sigma w}$$

Example:

```
portfolio_vol = np.sqrt(
np.dot(weights.T, np.dot(cov_matrix, weights))
)
```

Target volatility control:

```
if portfolio_vol > target_vol:
scale_down_positions()
```

Volatility targeting stabilizes portfolio risk across regimes.

5. Risk Contribution Analysis

Each asset contributes differently to total portfolio risk.

Marginal risk contribution:

$$\text{MRC}_i = w_i(\Sigma w)_i$$

Assets with large weights and high covariance dominate risk.

Equalizing risk contributions (risk parity) improves stability.

Example conceptual approach:

```
risk_contribution = weights * (cov_matrix @ weights)
```

Reduce weights where contribution is excessive.

6. Drawdown Control at Portfolio Level

Individual strategy drawdown may be manageable, but combined drawdown may exceed tolerance.

Monitor cumulative portfolio equity:

```
cumulative = (1 + portfolio_returns).cumprod()
drawdown = cumulative / cumulative.cummax() - 1
```

Portfolio-level rules:

- Reduce leverage after X% drawdown

- Pause high-risk strategies
- Shift capital to defensive allocation

Drawdown management must operate above strategy layer.

7. Tail Risk Aggregation

Individual strategies may have mild tail risk but share exposure to extreme events.

Example:

- Multiple strategies long equities
- All vulnerable to sudden market crash

Estimate portfolio VaR:

```
portfolio_var = np.percentile(portfolio_returns, 5)
```

Simulate stress scenarios:

- Historical crisis periods
- Volatility spikes
- Correlation breakdown

Stress testing reveals hidden vulnerabilities.

8. Liquidity Risk

Portfolio-level risk includes liquidity constraints.

If multiple strategies trade illiquid assets:

- Slippage increases
- Exit becomes difficult
- Market impact magnifies losses

Monitor:

- Average daily volume
- Position size relative to volume

Constraint example:

```
if position_size > 0.1 * avg_daily_volume:
```

reduce_position()

Liquidity-aware risk control is critical in multi-asset portfolios.

9. Leverage and Margin Risk

Total leverage must align with capital capacity.

Monitor:

- Gross leverage
- Margin utilization
- Stress-adjusted leverage

Example:

if gross_exposure > max_leverage:

scale_all_positions()

Leverage magnifies drawdowns nonlinearly.

10. Hierarchical Risk Control Framework

Effective portfolio risk control operates at three levels:

- Trade-level controls
- Strategy-level controls
- Portfolio-level controls

Portfolio layer overrides lower layers when needed.

Example emergency control:

if portfolio_drawdown < -0.2:

close_all_positions()

This kill-switch protects capital during extreme events.

11. Dynamic Risk Budgeting

Allocate total portfolio risk across strategies.

Example:

- **Strategy A:** 30% risk budget
- **Strategy B:** 40%

- **Strategy C:** 30%

If one strategy exceeds its risk budget:

if strategy_vol > allocated_risk:

reduce_weight()

Risk budgeting enforces disciplined diversification.

12. Monitoring and Automation

Portfolio-level risk control must be automated and real-time.

Monitor:

- Rolling volatility
- Correlation spikes
- Drawdown
- Exposure concentration
- Liquidity metrics

Risk alerts should trigger predefined actions.

Manual intervention is too slow in fast markets.

Practical Portfolio Risk Checklist

Before live deployment:

- Set gross and net exposure limits.
- Define max asset and sector concentration.
- Implement volatility targeting.
- Monitor correlation clustering.
- Stress-test crisis periods.
- Define drawdown thresholds and actions.
- Enforce liquidity constraints.

Portfolio-level discipline reduces catastrophic failure probability.

Final Principle

Individual strategies can be profitable yet collectively dangerous.

Portfolio-level risk control ensures that:

- Diversification is real, not assumed
- Correlation spikes are managed
- Tail events do not cause irreversible damage
- Leverage remains within survivable limits

Alpha generates return.

Portfolio risk control ensures continuity.

In systematic trading, survival is a portfolio-level property, not a strategy-level one.

Chapter 11: Execution Algorithms and Market Impact

Execution is where optimism goes to die quietly. Slippage, fees, and market impact turn theoretical profits into real losses. Ignoring execution is like designing a race car and forgetting friction exists.

This chapter explains execution strategies, transaction cost minimization, and intelligent order routing.

11.1 Order Execution Strategies and Slippage

Execution is where theoretical alpha meets market reality.

A strategy that looks profitable in backtests can lose money purely due to poor execution. Slippage, spread costs, and market impact quietly erode returns.

Execution is not an afterthought. It is part of the trading system.

This section focuses on:

- Types of order execution strategies
- Sources of slippage
- Modeling execution realistically
- Designing execution logic within agent systems

1. What Is Slippage?

Slippage is the difference between:

- Expected execution price
- Actual execution price

Example:

- You generate a buy signal at price = 100.
- Your order fills at 100.20.
- Slippage = +0.20.

Slippage comes from:

- Bid-ask spread
- Market impact
- Latency
- Liquidity shortages

Ignoring slippage invalidates backtests.

2. Basic Order Types

Execution strategy begins with order type selection.

2.1 Market Orders

Execute immediately at best available price.

Example:

place_order(symbol, quantity, order_type="market")

Advantages:

- Guaranteed fill (in liquid markets)
- Simplicity

Disadvantages:

- Pay spread
- Vulnerable to slippage
- Sensitive to market impact

Used when immediacy matters more than price precision.

2.2 Limit Orders

Specify maximum buy price or minimum sell price.

place_order(symbol, quantity, order_type="limit", price=target_price)

Advantages:

- Price control
- Reduced spread cost

Disadvantages:

- No fill guarantee
- Partial fills
- Opportunity cost

Used when patience is acceptable.

2.3 Stop Orders

Triggered when price crosses a threshold.

Often used for:

- Risk control
- Breakout strategies

Execution may occur at worse price during fast moves.

3. Spread and Its Impact

Bid-ask spread is a fundamental cost.

If spread is 0.10:

- Buy at ask
- Sell at bid
- Round-trip cost = spread.

For high-frequency strategies, spread dominates profitability.

Spread modeling example:

effective_price = mid_price + spread / 2

Backtests must simulate realistic spread assumptions.

4. Market Impact

Large orders move price.

Impact increases with:

- Order size
- Illiquidity
- Volatility

Simple impact model:

$$\text{Impact} \propto \frac{\text{Order Size}}{\text{Average Volume}}$$

Approximation:

*impact = k * (order_size / avg_daily_volume)*

Ignoring impact overestimates performance for scalable strategies.

5. Execution Algorithms

Execution strategies aim to minimize:

- Market impact
- Slippage
- Information leakage

Common algorithms:

5.1 TWAP (Time-Weighted Average Price)

Splits order evenly over time.

Example:

- Total order: 10,000 shares
- Execute 1,000 shares every minute

Reduces market impact.

Used for moderate urgency trades.

5.2 VWAP (Volume-Weighted Average Price)

Executes proportionally to market volume.

Heavier execution during high liquidity periods.

Better when volume patterns are predictable.

5.3 Participation Rate Strategy

Executes as a percentage of market volume.

Example:

target_participation = 0.05 # 5% of volume

Limits impact relative to liquidity.

5.4 Implementation Shortfall Strategy

Optimizes trade-off between:

- Speed
- Market impact

More aggressive early execution if price moves against position.

Often adaptive and data-driven.

6. Latency Considerations

Latency includes:

- Data delay
- Decision computation
- Order routing
- Exchange processing

For short-horizon strategies, latency is critical.

Simulate execution delay:

execution_price = price.shift(-1)

More realistic:

- Add random slippage
- Add spread cost
- Add time delay

Ignoring latency overestimates short-term alpha.

7. Execution in Multi-Agent Systems

Execution module should be independent from signal module.

Signal generates target position:

target_position = risk_module(signal)

Execution converts target to orders:

orders = execution_engine.generate_orders(

current_position,

target_position

)

Separation prevents execution assumptions from contaminating signal training.

8. Slippage Modeling in Backtesting

Minimum realistic model:

net_return = gross_return - spread - commission

More realistic model:

net_return = gross_return - spread - commission - impact_cost

Advanced simulation includes:

- Partial fills
- Randomized fill probability
- Order queue modeling

The more frequent the strategy, the more detailed the execution model must be.

9. Monitoring Execution Performance

After deployment, track:

- Realized slippage
- Fill rate
- Average execution delay
- Deviation from benchmark (VWAP or arrival price)

Compare expected vs actual slippage.

If execution quality deteriorates, strategy profitability declines.

10. Trade-Off Between Speed and Cost

Fast execution:

- Reduces signal decay
- Increases impact

Slow execution:

- Reduces impact
- Increases timing risk

Execution strategy must match:

- Signal half-life
- Market liquidity
- Strategy horizon

Short-lived signals require faster execution.

Longer-term strategies tolerate slower scheduling.

Practical Execution Checklist

Before deploying:

- Include spread and commission in backtest.
- Model market impact realistically.
- Simulate latency.
- Choose order type aligned with signal urgency.
- Monitor real-time slippage.
- Enforce liquidity constraints.

Execution errors can eliminate alpha faster than model degradation.

Final Principle

Alpha generation and execution are inseparable.

A strategy with strong predictive power but poor execution will underperform.

Execution strategies aim to:

- Minimize friction
- Preserve signal edge
- Control market impact

In systematic trading, execution is not operational detail.

It is the final transformation step that converts model output into realized return.

11.2 Minimizing Transaction Costs and Market Impact

Transaction costs are the most predictable source of loss in any trading system.
Unlike alpha, which is uncertain, costs are guaranteed.

In systematic trading, minimizing transaction costs and market impact is often more effective than marginally improving prediction accuracy.

This section focuses on:

- Components of transaction cost
- Modeling cost realistically
- Structural techniques to reduce turnover
- Execution-level impact minimization
- Portfolio-level cost control

1. Components of Transaction Costs

Transaction costs include:

Explicit costs

- Commission
- Exchange fees

Implicit costs

- Bid-ask spread
- Slippage
- Market impact
- Opportunity cost

Total cost per trade:

$$\text{Total Cost} = \text{Commission} + \text{Spread} + \text{Impact}$$

Ignoring implicit costs is the most common backtesting mistake.

2. Spread Cost

Every market order crosses the spread.

Approximate cost:

spread_cost = spread / 2

Round-trip cost:

round_trip_cost = spread

For high-frequency strategies, spread is often the dominant expense.

Reducing unnecessary trades directly improves performance.

3. Market Impact

Impact increases with order size relative to liquidity.

Simple impact approximation:

$$\text{Impact} \propto \frac{\text{Order Size}}{\text{Average Volume}}$$

Example:

*impact = k * (order_size / avg_daily_volume)*

Large positions in illiquid assets significantly increase cost.

Position size must respect liquidity constraints.

4. Reducing Turnover

The most powerful cost-reduction technique is lowering turnover.

Turnover:

turnover = abs(position.diff()).sum()

High turnover:

- Increases spread cost
- Increases impact
- Amplifies slippage

Techniques to reduce turnover:

4.1 Signal Smoothing

Instead of reacting instantly:

*smoothed_signal = 0.9 * previous_signal + 0.1 * new_signal*

Reduces unnecessary small adjustments.

4.2 Threshold Trading

Ignore weak signals.

if abs(signal) < threshold:

signal = 0

Prevents micro-trades that fail to cover costs.

4.3 Rebalancing Intervals

Instead of continuous rebalancing:

- Rebalance daily
- Rebalance weekly

Batch execution reduces transaction frequency.

5. Liquidity-Aware Position Sizing

Never size positions without considering volume.

Constraint example:

*max_position = 0.05 * avg_daily_volume*

position = min(target_position, max_position)

Limiting participation reduces market impact.

Scalable alpha must respect liquidity limits.

6. Order Splitting

Large orders should be divided into smaller slices.

Instead of:

execute(100000 shares)

Use:

- TWAP
- VWAP

- Participation rate strategies

Spreading execution reduces footprint.

7. Avoiding Adverse Selection

Adverse selection occurs when:

- You trade right before price moves against you.

Often caused by:

- Latency
- Predictable execution behavior
- Trading during illiquid conditions

Mitigation:

- Avoid trading during low liquidity windows
- Avoid predictable order timing
- Monitor fill quality

Execution timing matters.

8. Portfolio-Level Netting

Multiple strategies may generate offsetting trades.

Example:

- Strategy A wants +100
- Strategy B wants -100

Netting before execution reduces cost:

net_order = sum(strategy_orders)

Without netting, unnecessary round trips increase costs.

Centralized order management reduces redundant trades.

9. Adaptive Execution Based on Market Conditions

Execution aggressiveness should depend on:

- Spread

- Volatility
- Volume

Example:

if spread > threshold:

use_limit_orders()

else:

use_market_orders()

High-volatility regimes may require faster execution despite higher spread.

Adaptive execution balances urgency and cost.

10. Cost-Aware Signal Design

Signal generation should consider cost.

If expected return per trade:

$$E[r] < \text{Transaction Cost}$$

Do not trade.

Example:

if expected_return > cost_estimate:

trade()

Embedding cost threshold improves net performance.

11. Monitoring Realized Costs

After deployment, track:

- Average slippage
- Spread paid
- Participation rate
- Execution shortfall

Compare:

- Expected cost (backtest)

- Realized cost (live)

If discrepancy grows, recalibrate assumptions.

Cost drift often occurs during regime shifts.

12. Stress Testing Cost Sensitivity

Increase assumed transaction cost in backtests:

- +25%
- +50%

Observe performance degradation.

Robust strategies maintain profitability under conservative cost assumptions.

If small cost increase eliminates edge, signal is fragile.

13. Balancing Turnover and Alpha Decay

Trade-off:

- **Faster reaction** → higher turnover
- **Slower reaction** → signal decay

Optimization goal:

Maximize net alpha:

$$\text{Net Alpha} = \text{Gross Alpha} - \text{Cost}$$

In many cases, reducing turnover improves net Sharpe more than increasing prediction accuracy.

Practical Cost-Control Checklist

Before deployment:

- Include spread, commission, and impact in backtests.
- Apply liquidity constraints.
- Limit participation rate.
- Smooth signals to reduce micro-adjustments.
- Net orders across strategies.
- Stress-test cost assumptions.

Cost control is structural, not tactical.

Final Principle

Transaction costs are certain. Alpha is uncertain.

Minimizing transaction costs:

- Improves net performance
- Increases scalability
- Enhances robustness

Market impact grows nonlinearly with size.

Reducing turnover and respecting liquidity constraints are often more powerful than adding new predictive features.

In systematic trading, cost discipline converts fragile models into durable systems.

11.3 Timing, Scheduling, and Smart Order Routing

Execution quality depends not only on order type, but also on when and where orders are sent. Even if signal and position sizing are correct, poor timing or routing can significantly degrade realized performance.

This section focuses on:

- Timing decisions
- Order scheduling strategies
- Smart order routing (SOR)

Integrating execution intelligence into agent systems

Execution is not just price control. It is liquidity optimization.

1. Timing: When to Execute

Markets exhibit predictable intraday patterns:

- Higher liquidity at open and close
- Lower liquidity mid-session
- Volume spikes around macro announcements

Executing large trades during thin liquidity increases:

- Spread cost
- Market impact
- Slippage variance

1.1 Liquidity-Aware Timing

Example rule:

if current_volume > volume_threshold:

execute()

Better execution often occurs when liquidity is abundant.

1.2 Volatility-Aware Timing

High volatility may:

- Improve fill probability
- Increase price uncertainty

Adaptive rule:

if volatility < max_vol_threshold:

use_passive_execution()

else:

increase_aggressiveness()

Execution urgency should match signal half-life.

Short-lived signals require faster timing even if cost increases.

2. Order Scheduling Strategies

Scheduling divides large orders over time to reduce market impact.

2.1 TWAP (Time-Based Scheduling)

Divide order evenly across fixed time intervals.

Example:

slice_size = total_quantity / num_intervals

Advantages:

- Simple
- Predictable

Disadvantages:

- Ignores real-time liquidity conditions

Best used in stable liquidity environments.

2.2 VWAP (Volume-Based Scheduling)

Execute in proportion to observed market volume.

Heavier execution during high-volume periods.

Conceptually:

*slice_size = participation_rate * observed_volume*

Advantages:

- Adapts to liquidity
- Reduces impact

Better suited for institutional-scale orders.

2.3 Implementation Shortfall Scheduling

Balances urgency vs cost.

If price moves favorably, delay execution.

If price moves against position, accelerate.

Conceptually:

if adverse_move_detected:

increase_execution_speed()

Requires dynamic monitoring.

3. Smart Order Routing (SOR)

In fragmented markets (e.g., equities), multiple venues exist:

- Primary exchanges
- Alternative trading systems
- Dark pools

Smart order routing determines:

- Which venue to send the order to
- In what size
- In what sequence

Objective:

- Maximize fill quality while minimizing cost.

3.1 Routing Criteria

Factors influencing routing decisions:

- Best available price
- Available depth
- Historical fill quality

-
- Latency to venue
- Fee structure

Simplified routing logic:

best_venue = argmin(expected_execution_cost_per_venue)

3.2 Dark Pool Considerations

Dark pools offer:

- Reduced market impact
- Less price transparency

Risks:

- Partial fills
- Adverse selection

Often used for large blocks before routing to lit exchanges.

4. Participation Rate Control

Controlling participation reduces signaling risk.

Example:

participation_rate = 0.05 # 5% of volume

*order_size = participation_rate * market_volume*

Higher participation increases impact.

Lower participation reduces footprint but increases timing risk.

5. Latency and Routing

Routing delay increases:

- Opportunity cost
- Adverse selection risk

High-frequency strategies require:

- Low-latency data feeds
- Fast order acknowledgment

- Minimal routing hops

For longer-horizon strategies, microsecond latency is less critical.

Infrastructure must match strategy horizon.

6. Adaptive Execution in Agent Systems

Execution logic should not be static.

Example integration:

execution_mode = execution_policy(

volatility,

spread,

signal_urgency

)

Agent determines:

- Aggressiveness level
- Scheduling speed
- Venue priority

However, execution must remain within risk constraints.

Never allow signal model to bypass execution safeguards.

7. Avoiding Information Leakage

Large visible orders can signal intent to market participants.

Mitigation:

- Slice orders
- Randomize execution intervals
- Vary order size slightly
- Avoid predictable timing patterns

Predictable execution invites adverse price movement.

8. Monitoring Execution Performance

Key metrics:

- Implementation shortfall
- Slippage vs arrival price
- Fill rate
- Venue performance

Example:

shortfall = execution_price - decision_price

Track average shortfall over time.

Degrading routing quality reduces strategy edge.

9. Interaction with Risk Control

Execution speed affects portfolio risk.

Slow execution:

- Exposes portfolio to interim market risk

Fast execution:

- Increases impact

Balance must consider:

- Strategy half-life
- Market liquidity
- Risk tolerance

Risk and execution modules must communicate clearly.

10. Stress Testing Execution

Simulate:

- Liquidity collapse
- Spread widening
- Sudden volatility spike
- Venue outage

Execution resilience matters during extreme conditions.

Design fallback routing:

if primary_venue_unavailable:

route_to_secondary()

Operational robustness protects capital.

Practical Execution Timing Checklist

Before deployment:

- Define execution urgency per strategy.
- Model liquidity patterns.
- Implement order slicing logic.
- Apply participation constraints.
- Test routing logic across venues.
- Monitor implementation shortfall continuously.

Execution timing is not static configuration. It must adapt to environment.

Final Principle

Execution determines realized alpha.

Timing decides how much of the signal you preserve.

Scheduling controls how much impact you create.

Smart routing determines where liquidity is accessed efficiently.

In advanced trading systems, execution is not a backend process.

It is a dynamic optimization layer that protects edge and preserves capital under real market conditions.

Chapter 12: Backtesting and Simulation Frameworks

Backtests are liars unless proven otherwise. I've trusted backtests that looked flawless and failed instantly. This chapter is about forcing honesty into your simulations.

This chapter covers realistic backtesting design, bias prevention, stress testing, and Monte Carlo simulation.

12.1 Designing Realistic Backtests

Backtests are necessary. They are also dangerous.

A backtest is not proof of profitability. It is a simulation under assumptions. If those assumptions are unrealistic, results are meaningless.

Designing realistic backtests is one of the most important engineering tasks in systematic trading.

This section focuses on:

- Structural requirements of a realistic backtest
- Data integrity and alignment
- Execution and cost modeling
- Walk-forward methodology
- Stress testing and validation

The goal is honesty, not optimism.

1. Core Principles of Realistic Backtesting

A realistic backtest must:

- Use only information available at the time of decision
- Include transaction costs
- Model execution delay
- Reflect realistic liquidity constraints
- Avoid data leakage

If any of these are violated, results are inflated.

2. Chronological Integrity

Never shuffle time-series data.

Correct approach:

*split_index = int(len(data) * 0.7)*

train_data = data[:split_index]

test_data = data[split_index:]

All training, parameter tuning, and feature scaling must be based only on historical data preceding evaluation period.

Random cross-validation is invalid for financial time series.

3. Preventing Look-Ahead Bias

Look-ahead bias occurs when future information leaks into features.

Example mistake:

rolling_mean = price.rolling(20).mean()

signal = price > rolling_mean

If not shifted:

rolling_mean = price.rolling(20).mean().shift(1)

All rolling statistics must be shifted.

Economic data must use release timestamps, not revised values.

Backtest realism begins with correct temporal alignment.

4. Realistic Execution Modeling

Backtests must simulate how trades are filled.

At minimum, include:

- Bid-ask spread
- Commission
- Slippage

Example:

net_return = gross_return - spread - commission

For intraday systems:

- Model execution delay
- Use next-bar price instead of same-bar price

Example:

execution_price = price.shift(-1)

Better simulations incorporate:

- Partial fills

- Liquidity limits
- Market impact

Execution modeling should match strategy horizon.

5. Transaction Cost Sensitivity

After including baseline cost assumptions, increase them.

Example:

- Base cost
- +25% cost
- +50% cost

If performance collapses under modest cost increases, strategy is fragile.

Robust strategies tolerate conservative cost assumptions.

6. Liquidity Constraints

Ensure position size is realistic relative to market volume.

Example:

*max_position = 0.05 * avg_daily_volume*

position = min(target_position, max_position)

Backtests that ignore liquidity implicitly assume infinite market depth.

This is rarely true.

7. Walk-Forward Testing

Instead of single train-test split, use rolling windows.

Procedure:

- Train on window A
- Test on window B
- Slide forward
- Repeat

Aggregate results across all test windows.

This simulates real deployment conditions.

Hyperparameter tuning must occur inside each training window.

8. Parameter Stability Analysis

Test performance across nearby parameter values.

Example:

for lookback in [15, 20, 25]:

test_strategy(lookback)

If performance only works at exactly 21-day lookback and fails elsewhere, strategy is likely overfitted.

Robust strategies show gradual performance variation across parameter ranges.

9. Out-of-Sample Holdout Period

Reserve a final holdout dataset that is never used during development.

After finalizing strategy:

- Run one evaluation on holdout
- Do not adjust model afterward

If you adjust after seeing holdout results, it becomes in-sample.

Discipline matters.

10. Stress Testing

Test under extreme historical periods:

- Financial crises
- Volatility spikes
- Liquidity shocks

Simulate:

- Spread widening
- Latency increase
- Correlation spikes

Backtests should include worst-case conditions.

Ignoring stress conditions produces fragile systems.

11. Turnover and Capacity Analysis

Monitor:

turnover = abs(position.diff()).sum()

High turnover increases cost sensitivity.

Also evaluate capacity:

- Does performance degrade when scaling position size?
- Is impact manageable at larger allocations?

Scalable alpha is more valuable than narrow capacity strategies.

12. Avoiding Data Mining Bias

Common trap:

- Repeatedly modifying strategy after observing backtest results.
- Each iteration increases overfitting probability.

Best practice:

- Maintain research log
- Define hypothesis before testing
- Limit number of parameter variations

Discipline reduces false discoveries.

13. Performance Evaluation Metrics

Backtest evaluation must include:

- Net return after costs
- Sharpe ratio
- Maximum drawdown
- Drawdown duration
- Tail risk metrics

High return alone is insufficient.

Evaluate stability across subperiods.

14. Code Structure for Backtesting

Separate modules:

features = feature_engineer(data)

signals = model.predict(features)

positions = risk_manager(signals)

returns = execution_engine(positions, data)

Modular backtests reduce accidental leakage.

Use same preprocessing pipeline in research and production.

Practical Backtesting Checklist

Before trusting results:

- No look-ahead bias.
- Transaction costs included.
- Execution delay modeled.
- Liquidity constraints applied.
- Walk-forward testing completed.
- Parameter sensitivity tested.
- Stress tests performed.
- Holdout period evaluated.

If any are missing, results are optimistic.

Final Principle

Backtests do not predict the future.

They test whether a strategy survives realistic assumptions.

A good backtest is conservative, transparent, and disciplined.

A bad backtest is optimized, unrealistic, and impressive.

In systematic trading, realistic backtesting is not about maximizing historical return.

It is about minimizing unpleasant surprises in live markets.

12.2 Avoiding Look-Ahead and Data Leakage Bias

Look-ahead bias and data leakage are the most dangerous hidden errors in systematic trading research.

- They do not cause small mistakes.
- They create entirely fictional alpha.

Many strategies that fail in live trading were never valid in the first place. They were trained on information that would not have been available at decision time.

This section focuses on:

- What look-ahead and leakage mean in trading
- Common sources of leakage
- Structural safeguards
- Implementation discipline

The goal is temporal integrity.

1. What Is Look-Ahead Bias?

Look-ahead bias occurs when a model uses information from the future to make decisions about the past.

Example:

- At time t, you generate a signal using data from time t+1.

This invalidates the backtest.

Common symptom:

- Exceptional backtest performance that collapses in live trading.

2. What Is Data Leakage?

Data leakage is broader than look-ahead bias.

It occurs when:

- Training data indirectly contains information about validation or test data.
- Features embed future information through preprocessing.
- Target information contaminates inputs.

Leakage can occur even if timestamps appear correct.

3. Common Sources of Look-Ahead Bias

3.1 Rolling Statistics Without Shifting

Incorrect:

rolling_mean = price.rolling(20).mean()

signal = price > rolling_mean

Correct:

rolling_mean = price.rolling(20).mean().shift(1)

Without shifting, the current price influences its own prediction.

3.2 Using Closing Price Before Market Close

If your strategy trades intraday but uses same-day closing price for signal, you are cheating.

Signal must only use data available before execution.

3.3 Future Return Alignment Errors

Incorrect:

data["future_return"] = price.pct_change(5)

CORRECT:

data["future_return"] = price.pct_change(5).shift(-5)

Improper alignment silently corrupts training.

4. Common Sources of Data Leakage

4.1 Scaling on Entire Dataset

Incorrect:

scaler.fit(data)

scaled = scaler.transform(data)

Correct:

scaler.fit(train_data)

scaled_train = scaler.transform(train_data)

scaled_test = scaler.transform(test_data)

Scaling on full dataset leaks information from future into training.

4.2 Feature Selection on Entire Dataset

If you compute feature importance using all historical data before splitting into train/test, you are leaking information.

Feature selection must be performed inside training window only.

4.3 Hyperparameter Tuning on Test Set

Repeatedly tuning hyperparameters based on test results converts test data into training data.

Final evaluation must use untouched holdout set.

4.4 Using Revised Macroeconomic Data

Macroeconomic series are often revised.

If backtest uses final revised values rather than first-released values, it assumes perfect hindsight.

Always use release-date aligned data.

4.5 Survivorship Bias in Asset Universe

Using today's index constituents for past data excludes bankrupt or delisted companies.

This creates upward bias.

Historical universe must reflect assets available at that time.

5. Structural Safeguards

Prevent leakage by design.

5.1 Strict Time-Based Splitting

Never randomly shuffle financial data.

Correct structure:

train = data[:train_end]

validation = data[train_end:val_end]

test = data[val_end:]

All preprocessing steps must respect this split.

5.2 Walk-Forward Validation

For each window:

- Train on past
- Validate on future
- Slide forward

Feature selection and scaling must be re-computed inside each training window.

5.3 Encapsulated Pipelines

Use structured pipelines:

def train_pipeline(train_data):

scaler.fit(train_data)

model.fit(scaled_train)

return trained_model

Keep training and inference strictly separated.

5.4 Explicit Lagging of All Features

Rule:

- Every feature must represent information available strictly before decision time.

Safer pattern:

features = compute_features(data)

features = features.shift(1)

Then align with target.

6. Automated Leakage Detection

Implement sanity checks.

Example:

- Shuffle target randomly and re-train.
- If performance remains strong, leakage likely exists.

Another test:

- Shift features by large lag.
- Performance should degrade significantly.

If not, model may be exploiting leakage.

7. Validation Discipline

Never inspect test set results repeatedly.

Best practice:

- Develop on training and validation.
- Lock model.
- Evaluate once on test.

After seeing test results, do not adjust and re-test without creating new holdout.

Professional discipline separates research from confirmation bias.

8. Real-Time Simulation Mindset

Ask for every feature:

Would this value have been known at that exact timestamp?

If unsure, assume it would not.

Simulate real-time computation environment.

For example:

- Rolling windows computed incrementally.
- Macro data inserted only after release timestamp.

Backtest environment must mirror production environment.

9. Code Review and Logging

Leakage often hides in subtle alignment bugs.

Best practice:

- Log timestamps for every feature and target.
- Unit test feature alignment.
- Verify no negative lag exists in feature index.

Example assertion:

assert all(feature_timestamp <= decision_timestamp)

Engineering rigor reduces silent errors.

10. Psychological Discipline

Data leakage often results from:

- Optimism
- Confirmation bias
- Repeated tuning

When performance looks unusually strong, assume error first.

In trading research, skepticism protects capital.

Practical Leakage Prevention Checklist

Before trusting backtest:

- All rolling features shifted.
- Scaling applied only to training data.
- Feature selection inside training window.
- Hyperparameter tuning isolated from test data.
- Macro data aligned to release timestamps.
- Historical asset universe correctly constructed.
- Walk-forward validation performed.
- Holdout dataset untouched until final evaluation.

If any of these fail, backtest is unreliable.

Final Principle

Look-ahead bias and data leakage do not slightly inflate performance.

They manufacture it.

The market does not reward hindsight.

A strategy that depends on leaked information is not slightly flawed. It is invalid.

In systematic trading, temporal integrity is foundational.

If the system cannot replicate real-time decision constraints, it is not a backtest.

It is a historical illusion.

12.3 Monte Carlo Simulation and Stress Testing

A single historical backtest is one path through time.

Monte Carlo simulation and stress testing ask a more important question:

How sensitive is this strategy to randomness, sequencing, and extreme conditions?

If performance collapses under small perturbations, the strategy is fragile.

This section focuses on:

- Monte Carlo resampling
- Path dependency analysis
- Parameter stress testing
- Crisis scenario simulation
- Robustness interpretation

The objective is not to prove strength. It is to reveal weakness.

1. Why Monte Carlo Matters

Financial returns are path-dependent.

Even with identical average return and volatility:

- Different trade sequences produce different drawdowns.
- Early losses reduce capital and compounding ability.

Monte Carlo simulation helps answer:

- How variable is performance?
- What is worst-case drawdown under plausible variation?
- How sensitive is Sharpe ratio to randomness?

If small changes in order sequence destroy performance, edge is unstable.

2. Bootstrap Resampling of Returns

Simplest Monte Carlo method:

Resample historical returns with replacement.

Example:

import numpy as np

boot_returns = np.random.choice(strategy_returns,

size=len(strategy_returns),

replace=True)

cumulative = (1 + boot_returns).cumprod()

Repeat many times:

sharpe_list = []

max_dd_list = []

for _ in range(1000):

sample = np.random.choice(strategy_returns,

size=len(strategy_returns),

replace=True)

sharpe = sample.mean() / sample.std()

sharpe_list.append(sharpe)

This generates distribution of outcomes.

Interpretation:

- **Wide dispersion** → unstable strategy
- **Narrow dispersion** → more robust

3. Trade-Level Monte Carlo

Instead of daily returns, resample individual trades.

Procedure:

- Extract trade-level PnL.
- Randomize trade order.
- Recompute equity curve.

This isolates sequencing risk.

Even profitable strategies can experience deep drawdowns under unlucky trade ordering.

Understanding worst-case path is critical for risk planning.

4. Block Bootstrapping

Simple resampling breaks temporal correlation.

Markets exhibit:

- Volatility clustering
- Regime persistence

Block bootstrap preserves structure.

Example:

block_size = 20

Sample contiguous blocks instead of individual days.

This maintains regime patterns while randomizing sequence.

More realistic than naive resampling.

5. Parameter Sensitivity Stress Testing

Test robustness across parameter ranges.

Example:

for lookback in range(15, 31):

evaluate_strategy(lookback)

Plot performance surface.

If performance only exists at one narrow parameter value, strategy is likely overfitted.

Robust strategies show plateau-like behavior across parameter space.

6. Transaction Cost Stress Testing

Increase cost assumptions.

Example:

- Base spread
- +25% spread
- +50% spread

Recalculate net performance.

If Sharpe collapses under modest cost increase, edge is thin.

Cost robustness is essential for scalability.

7. Volatility Shock Simulation

Simulate sudden volatility increase.

Example:

*stress_returns = returns * 1.5*

Or insert historical high-volatility periods (e.g., crisis months).

Evaluate:

- Maximum drawdown
- Margin usage
- Leverage stress

If volatility spike causes forced liquidation in simulation, strategy is over-leveraged.

8. Correlation Breakdown Testing

In multi-asset portfolios, correlations rise during crises.

Simulate correlation shock:

- Increase covariance matrix off-diagonal elements
- Recalculate portfolio volatility

If diversification disappears under stress, portfolio risk is underestimated.

Correlation stress testing is essential for portfolio-level robustness.

9. Liquidity Stress Testing

Simulate:

- Reduced volume
- Wider spreads
- Increased impact coefficient

Example:

impact_multiplier = 2.0

Recompute execution cost.

If profitability depends on stable liquidity, scaling risk is high.

Liquidity collapses during crises.

10. Worst-Case Path Analysis

From Monte Carlo runs, extract:

- Worst 5% Sharpe
- Worst drawdown
- Worst cumulative return

Compare to acceptable risk tolerance.

Even if average simulation is strong, tail scenarios matter.

Capital allocation should reflect worst credible outcome, not average.

11. Confidence Intervals for Performance

Compute distribution of Sharpe ratios:

np.percentile(sharpe_list, [5, 50, 95])

If 5th percentile Sharpe is near zero or negative, edge is uncertain.

Investable strategies require statistical confidence, not just point estimates.

12. Integration into Research Workflow

Monte Carlo and stress testing should occur:

- After initial backtest
- Before deployment
- Periodically during live trading

It is not a one-time validation step.

Robustness is an ongoing requirement.

Practical Stress Testing Checklist

Before deployment:

- Bootstrap daily returns.
- Shuffle trade order.
- Apply block bootstrapping.

- Vary parameters within reasonable ranges.
- Increase transaction cost assumptions.
- Simulate volatility and correlation shocks.
- Evaluate worst-case drawdown scenarios.

If strategy survives conservative assumptions, confidence increases.

If it fails under modest stress, redesign is required.

Final Principle

Backtests show what happened.

Monte Carlo and stress testing show what could happen.

Financial markets are uncertain and nonlinear.

A strategy that only works under one historical path is fragile.

A robust strategy:

- Maintains performance under random sequencing
- Survives parameter perturbations
- Tolerates cost increases
- Endures volatility spikes

The objective is not perfect prediction.

It is durable performance under uncertainty.

Stress testing transforms optimistic backtests into realistic expectations.

Chapter 13: Evaluation and Performance Attribution

When something breaks, guessing is expensive. I learned that knowing why an agent made money or lost money matters more than the result itself.

This chapter introduces performance metrics, attribution analysis, and methods for detecting strategy degradation.

13.1 Performance Metrics and Benchmarking

- A strategy that makes money is not necessarily good.
- A strategy that outperforms appropriately measured alternatives might be.

Performance evaluation requires two elements:

- Proper metrics
- Proper benchmarks

Without benchmarking, you do not know whether your strategy adds value or merely captures general market exposure.

This section focuses on practical evaluation standards for professional trading systems.

1. Absolute Return Metrics

Absolute metrics measure standalone performance.

1.1 Cumulative Return

Total compounded return:

cumulative_return = (1 + returns).cumprod() - 1

This shows growth but ignores risk.

High cumulative return with extreme volatility is not necessarily desirable.

1.2 Annualized Return

*annual_return = (1 + returns).prod() ** (252 / len(returns)) - 1*

Standardizes return across different time horizons.

Must always be interpreted alongside risk metrics.

2. Risk-Adjusted Metrics

Risk-adjusted metrics evaluate efficiency of return generation.

2.1 Sharpe Ratio

$$\text{Sharpe} = \frac{E[R]}{\sigma}$$

Example:

sharpe = returns.mean() / returns.std()

*annual_sharpe = sharpe * np.sqrt(252)*

Measures return per unit of volatility.

Widely used but assumes symmetric distribution.

2.2 Sortino Ratio

Penalizes only downside volatility:

downside_std = returns[returns < 0].std()

sortino = returns.mean() / downside_std

More appropriate for asymmetric strategies.

2.3 Calmar Ratio

$$\text{Calmar} = \frac{\text{Annual Return}}{\text{Max Drawdown}}$$

Measures return relative to worst capital decline.

Useful for capital preservation strategies.

3. Drawdown Metrics

Return without drawdown analysis is incomplete.

3.1 Maximum Drawdown

cumulative = (1 + returns).cumprod()

drawdown = cumulative / cumulative.cummax() - 1

max_dd = drawdown.min()

Critical for understanding capital risk.

3.2 Drawdown Duration

Length of time required to recover from loss.

Long recovery periods can be more problematic than deep but brief drawdowns.

4. Trade-Level Metrics

For higher-frequency strategies:

- Win rate
- Average win
- Average loss
- Profit factor

Profit factor:

profit_factor = gross_profit / abs(gross_loss)

High win rate alone is misleading.

Risk-reward balance matters more.

5. Benchmarking

Absolute performance is insufficient.

Benchmark answers:

- Is this strategy better than doing nothing or holding a passive alternative?

5.1 Market Benchmark

For equity strategies:

- Compare to broad index return.

Excess return:

excess_return = strategy_return - benchmark_return

If strategy behaves like leveraged index exposure, alpha may be minimal.

5.2 Risk-Free Benchmark

Sharpe ratio often uses risk-free rate as baseline.

Excess return:

$$R_{excess} = R_{strategy} - R_{risk-free}$$

For short-term systems, risk-free may be small but should be included for completeness.

5.3 Factor Benchmarking

Strategies may unknowingly load on common risk factors:

- Market beta
- Size
- Value
- Momentum

Estimate beta:

*beta = np.cov(strategy_returns, benchmark_returns)[0, 1] / *

np.var(benchmark_returns)

If beta is high, returns may reflect market exposure rather than true alpha.

Risk-adjusted alpha:

$$\alpha = R_{strategy} - \beta R_{benchmark}$$

True alpha should persist after factor adjustment.

6. Rolling Performance Analysis

Static metrics hide instability.

Compute rolling Sharpe:

*rolling_sharpe = returns.rolling(252).mean() / *

returns.rolling(252).std()

Track:

- Stability
- Regime sensitivity
- Degradation over time

Consistent rolling performance indicates robustness.

7. Cross-Regime Benchmarking

Evaluate performance in:

- Bull markets
- Bear markets
- High-volatility regimes

- Low-volatility regimes

A strategy outperforming only in one regime may not justify capital allocation.

Conditional benchmarking improves understanding of structural strengths.

8. Capacity and Scalability Metrics

Beyond performance:

- Turnover
- Slippage sensitivity
- Liquidity constraints

High Sharpe with low capacity may not be scalable.

Monitor:

turnover = abs(position.diff()).sum()

Performance must be evaluated net of realistic execution constraints.

9. Statistical Confidence

Estimate confidence intervals for Sharpe:

Bootstrap example:

boot_sample = np.random.choice(returns,

size=len(returns),

replace=True)

Compute Sharpe distribution.

If lower percentile Sharpe is near zero, confidence in edge is weak.

Point estimate is insufficient.

10. Monitoring Live vs Backtest Drift

Compare:

- Live Sharpe vs backtest Sharpe
- Realized slippage vs modeled slippage
- Rolling beta vs historical beta

Deviations may indicate:

- Regime shift
- Model decay
- Execution issues

Performance evaluation continues after deployment.

Practical Performance Evaluation Checklist

Before deploying capital:

- Evaluate net return after costs.
- Calculate Sharpe, Sortino, and Calmar.
- Measure max drawdown and duration.
- Compare against relevant benchmark.
- Estimate beta and risk-adjusted alpha.
- Analyze rolling stability.
- Assess turnover and scalability.
- Compute confidence intervals via bootstrap.

If performance only looks strong relative to no benchmark, edge may be illusory.

Final Principle

- Performance metrics quantify outcomes.
- Benchmarking provides context.
- Without benchmarking, you measure growth.
- With benchmarking, you measure value added.

Professional trading systems must demonstrate:

- Risk-adjusted superiority
- Stability across regimes
- Independence from passive market exposure

True alpha is performance that remains after accounting for risk, cost, and market beta.

Anything else is exposure disguised as skill.

13.2 Attribution Analysis for Agent Decisions

When a trading agent makes or loses money, the most important question is not how much, but why.
Attribution analysis decomposes performance into interpretable components:

- Signal contribution
- Risk allocation impact
- Execution effects
- Market exposure
- Regime influence

Without attribution, improvement becomes guesswork. With attribution, system refinement becomes structured engineering.

1. Why Attribution Matters

Consider two scenarios:

- Strategy generates profit due to strong signal quality.
- Strategy generates profit due to rising market beta exposure.
- Both show positive returns. Only one represents true alpha.

Attribution separates:

- Skill
- Structural exposure
- Random luck
- Execution effects

Professional systems must explain performance, not just report it.

2. Return Decomposition Framework

Basic portfolio return:

$$R_t = \sum_i w_{i,t} r_{i,t}$$

RETURN ATTRIBUTION decomposes this into:

- Allocation effect
- Selection effect
- Interaction effect

At strategy level, a simplified decomposition is:

$$\text{Total Return} = \text{Signal Return} - \text{Transaction Cost} + \text{Beta Exposure}$$

Each component must be measured independently.

3. Signal vs Execution Attribution

Separate signal return from execution return.

3.1 Theoretical Signal Return

Compute return assuming ideal execution at mid-price.

*theoretical_return = signal.shift(1) * future_return*

3.2 Realized Return

realized_return = net_strategy_return

Execution impact:

execution_effect = realized_return - theoretical_return

If execution effect is consistently negative and large, slippage is degrading performance.

4. Allocation Attribution

In multi-strategy portfolios, performance may depend on capital allocation.

Decompose:

*strategy_contribution = weight * strategy_return*

Analyze:

- Which strategy contributed most
- Which strategy consumed most risk
- Whether allocation amplified volatility

Allocation layer may improve or degrade total performance independent of signal quality.

5. Factor Exposure Attribution

Agents may unknowingly load on systematic factors.

Estimate regression:

$$R_{strategy} = \alpha + \beta R_{market} + \epsilon$$

Example:

```
beta = np.cov(strategy_returns, benchmark_returns)[0,1] / \
np.var(benchmark_returns)
```

Alpha component:

$$\alpha = R_{strategy} - \beta R_{benchmark}$$

If most return is explained by beta, agent is not generating independent alpha.

Factor attribution improves clarity.

6. Risk Contribution Attribution

Determine which positions contribute most to portfolio risk.

Marginal risk contribution:

$$\text{MRC}_i = w_i(\Sigma w)_i$$

Example:

```
risk_contribution = weights * (cov_matrix @ weights)
```

High return from one asset may also carry disproportionate risk.

Risk attribution prevents hidden concentration.

7. Regime-Based Attribution

Segment returns by regime.

Example:

```
returns_high_vol = returns[regime == 1]
```

returns_low_vol = returns[regime == 0]

Analyze:

- Sharpe in high-vol regime
- Sharpe in low-vol regime

A strategy profitable only in one regime may require adaptive weighting.

Regime attribution helps refine adaptive logic.

8. Trade-Level Attribution

Decompose performance by trade characteristics:

- Long vs short
- Large vs small positions
- High-confidence vs low-confidence signals
- Time-of-day performance

Example:

long_return = returns[positions > 0].mean()

short_return = returns[positions < 0].mean()

If only one side generates alpha, strategy may require directional bias adjustment.

9. Model Feature Attribution

For ML-based agents, interpret model decisions.

For linear models:

*contribution = feature_value * model_coefficient*

For tree-based models, use feature importance metrics.

For neural networks, use:

- SHAP values
- Integrated gradients

Understanding feature contribution helps detect:

- Spurious correlations
- Overfitting

- Regime sensitivity

Model interpretability improves system trustworthiness.

10. Timing Attribution

Measure performance by holding period.

Example:

return_1d = compute_return(horizon=1)

return_5d = compute_return(horizon=5)

If signal performs only over short horizon but execution delays are long, timing mismatch exists.

Timing attribution aligns signal half-life with execution strategy.

11. Error Attribution

Analyze losing periods:

- Were losses driven by regime shift?
- Increased volatility?
- Cost expansion?
- Correlation spike?

Compare predicted vs realized return:

prediction_error = predicted_return - realized_return

Persistent bias indicates model degradation.

Attribution is not only for profits.

It is more valuable during losses.

12. Attribution Reporting Structure

Professional reporting includes:

- Total return
- Allocation contribution
- Signal contribution
- Cost impact
- Factor exposure

- Regime breakdown
- Risk contribution

Structured reporting enables informed adjustments.

13. Live Monitoring Attribution

In production:

- Track rolling alpha vs benchmark
- Monitor beta drift
- Monitor cost drift
- Monitor regime-specific performance

If performance shifts structurally, attribution identifies source quickly.

Without attribution, troubleshooting becomes reactive and slow.

Practical Attribution Checklist

After each evaluation period:

- Separate theoretical vs realized return.
- Decompose allocation vs selection effects.
- Estimate factor exposures.
- Measure risk contributions.
- Analyze regime-specific performance.
- Inspect feature-level importance.
- Compare prediction vs outcome error.
- Attribution must be routine, not occasional.

Final Principle

Performance answers "how much."

Attribution answers "why."

Without attribution, improvement is blind iteration.

With attribution, system refinement becomes targeted and controlled.

In autonomous trading systems, explainability is not optional.

Understanding why an agent makes money is as important as the money itself.

Durable systems are interpretable systems.

13.3 Detecting Strategy Decay and Failure Modes

No strategy remains optimal forever.

Markets evolve. Participants adapt. Liquidity shifts. Regulations change. A strategy that once generated consistent alpha can slowly degrade or fail abruptly.

The objective is not to prevent decay entirely. It is to detect it early and respond systematically.

This section focuses on:

- Types of strategy decay
- Statistical detection methods
- Monitoring signals of degradation
- Structural failure modes
- Response frameworks

A professional trading system must assume eventual decay.

1. Types of Strategy Decay

Strategy degradation typically falls into three categories:

1.1 Gradual Decay

- Rolling Sharpe slowly declines
- Signal correlation with returns weakens
- Alpha becomes inconsistent

Often caused by:

- Crowding
- Structural market changes
- Regime evolution

1.2 Sudden Breakdown

- Sharp drawdown
- Unexpected loss clustering

- Correlation spike

Often linked to:

- Regime shift
- Liquidity shock
- Model instability

1.3 Structural Obsolescence

- Edge disappears permanently
- Feature relationships invert
- Strategy becomes anti-correlated

This often occurs when:

- Market participants arbitrage the signal
- Microstructure changes eliminate inefficiency
- Understanding the type of decay guides response.

2. Monitoring Rolling Performance Metrics

Continuous monitoring is essential.

2.1 Rolling Sharpe Ratio

*rolling_sharpe = returns.rolling(252).mean() / *

returns.rolling(252).std()

If rolling Sharpe remains negative for extended period, investigate.

2.2 Rolling Information Coefficient (IC)

For signal-based systems:

rolling_ic = signal.rolling(252).corr(future_return)

Declining IC often precedes return degradation.

Signal decay appears before portfolio-level collapse.

3. Drawdown Analysis

Monitor:

- Depth

- Duration
- Frequency

If drawdowns:

- Become deeper than historical worst case
- Last significantly longer

Then structural change may have occurred.

Compare live drawdown distribution to historical Monte Carlo simulations.

If outside expected range, investigate.

4. Prediction Error Monitoring

Compare predicted vs realized returns:

prediction_error = predicted_return - realized_return

Track bias:

error_mean = prediction_error.rolling(100).mean()

Persistent bias suggests model miscalibration.

If model systematically overestimates returns, retraining may be required.

5. Regime-Specific Performance Drift

Segment performance by regime.

Example:

performance_by_regime = returns.groupby(regime).mean()

If strategy underperforms in regime where it historically succeeded, structural relationship may have changed.

Regime-aware systems must monitor conditional performance.

6. Factor Exposure Drift

Estimate rolling beta:

*rolling_beta = rolling_cov(strategy_returns, benchmark_returns) / *

rolling_var(benchmark_returns)

Unexpected beta increase indicates:

- Hidden directional exposure

- Allocation imbalance
- Structural shift

Alpha may deteriorate while beta dominates returns.

7. Cost and Execution Drift

Monitor:

- Slippage
- Spread cost
- Participation rate

If realized costs increase beyond modeled expectations, profitability declines even if signal quality remains stable.

Cost drift is often mistaken for alpha decay.

8. Correlation Drift in Multi-Strategy Portfolios

Strategies may become increasingly correlated.

rolling_corr = returns_df.rolling(60).corr()

Rising correlation reduces diversification benefit and increases portfolio risk.

Decay may occur at portfolio level even if individual strategies remain stable.

9. Statistical Breakpoint Detection

Use statistical tests to detect structural breaks.

Examples:

- Rolling t-statistic
- Chow test for parameter stability
- CUSUM (cumulative sum) test

Conceptually:

If parameter relationships change significantly, model assumptions are invalid.

Formal break detection improves objectivity.

10. Crowding Indicators

Signals may decay due to overcrowding.

Indicators include:

- Increased correlation with peer strategies
- Reduced edge after publication
- Faster signal decay over time

Crowded strategies often exhibit:

- Lower forward returns
- Higher volatility of returns

Monitoring crowding reduces surprise decay.

11. Early Warning Thresholds

Define quantitative triggers:

Example:

```
if rolling_sharpe < 0 for 3 consecutive months:
reduce_allocation()
```

Or:

```
if drawdown < -1.5 * historical_max_drawdown:
pause_strategy()
```

Thresholds must be defined before failure occurs.

Reactive decision-making introduces bias.

12. Failure Mode Classification

When decay occurs, classify root cause:

- Model misspecification
- Regime shift
- Execution degradation
- Liquidity shift
- Overfitting exposure
- Crowding

Diagnosis determines response:

- Retrain

- Reduce leverage
- Redesign features
- Replace strategy

Avoid immediate full abandonment without structured analysis.

13. Controlled Deactivation

If decay confirmed:

Gradual capital reduction:

*allocation *= 0.5*

Avoid abrupt liquidation unless systemic risk present.

Allow strategy to continue at lower risk while monitoring recovery.

Some decay is cyclical, not structural.

14. Continuous Learning Systems

For adaptive systems:

- Schedule periodic retraining
- Use rolling window data
- Validate post-retraining performance

However, retraining should not be automatic response to short-term noise.

Excessive retraining increases instability.

Practical Monitoring Framework

Daily:

- Update rolling Sharpe
- Monitor drawdown
- Track cost metrics

Weekly:

- Evaluate IC stability
- Check regime performance

Monthly:

- Review factor exposure
- Assess correlation shifts
- Compare live vs backtest drift

Structured monitoring reduces emotional reactions.

Final Principle

- Strategy decay is inevitable.

The question is not whether decay will occur, but whether it will be detected early.

Robust systems:

- Continuously monitor performance drivers
- Separate signal decay from cost drift
- Distinguish regime effects from structural failure
- Apply predefined de-risking rules

Failure is expensive.

Undetected failure is catastrophic.

In systematic trading, monitoring and decay detection are as important as alpha discovery.

Durability depends on disciplined response to changing conditions.

Chapter 14: Deployment and Infrastructure

Deploying agents felt like releasing something into the wild. Suddenly latency matters. Logs matter. Monitoring matters. Everything matters more than it did in development.

This chapter discusses production architecture, reliability, scalability, and live system monitoring.

14.1 System Architecture for Live Trading

A research notebook is not a trading system.

Live trading requires an architecture that is:

- Reliable
- Low-latency (when needed)
- Fault-tolerant
- Observable
- Risk-controlled

In production, small engineering mistakes become financial losses. Architecture is not infrastructure overhead. It is capital protection.

This section outlines a practical architecture for deploying AI trading agents in live markets.

1. Core Architectural Principles

A live trading system must satisfy five requirements:

- Deterministic decision flow
- Strict separation of concerns
- Real-time risk control
- Monitoring and observability
- Failure recovery mechanisms

Without these, even strong models fail in production.

2. High-Level System Components

A production trading architecture typically contains:

- Data Ingestion Layer
- Feature & State Engine
- Model Inference Engine
- Risk & Allocation Engine
- Execution Engine

- Portfolio & State Store
- Monitoring & Logging Layer

Each component should be modular and independently testable.

3. Data Ingestion Layer

Responsibilities:

- Market data feed handling
- Timestamp normalization
- Order book updates
- Corporate action adjustments
- Economic data ingestion

Critical properties:

- Low-latency processing
- Redundant data feeds
- Failover capability

Data must be validated before entering the system.

Example validation:

if price <= 0:

discard_tick()

Garbage data in live trading causes real losses.

4. Feature and State Engine

Transforms raw data into model-ready inputs.

Responsibilities:

- Rolling statistics
- Feature normalization
- Regime detection
- Portfolio state integration

Important constraint:

The production feature pipeline must match the research pipeline exactly.

Mismatch between research and production pipelines is a common failure mode.

5. Model Inference Engine

Handles real-time predictions.

Responsibilities:

- Load trained models
- Run inference efficiently
- Apply fallback logic

Example:

prediction = model.predict(features)

Requirements:

- Deterministic behavior
- Version-controlled models
- Graceful degradation if model fails

If inference fails:

use_safe_default_position()

Never allow model crash to leave portfolio unmanaged.

6. Risk and Allocation Engine

Risk control must override model output.

Responsibilities:

- Position limits
- Leverage constraints
- Exposure control
- Drawdown monitoring

Example override:

if portfolio_drawdown < -0.15:

reduce_positions()

Risk engine must operate independently of signal model.

Hard constraints should not depend on learned behavior.

7. Execution Engine

Translates target positions into executable orders.

Responsibilities:

- Order slicing
- Venue routing
- Participation rate control
- Fill monitoring

Example:

orders = execution_engine.generate_orders(

current_position,

target_position

)

EXECUTION MUST INCLUDE:

- Acknowledgment tracking
- Partial fill handling
- Cancel/replace logic

Failure in execution layer can accumulate unintended exposure.

8. Portfolio State Store

Maintains authoritative system state:

- Positions
- Cash balance
- Exposure
- Realized and unrealized PnL

State must be:

- Persisted
- Recoverable
- Consistent across components

Inconsistent state is a critical failure risk.

9. Monitoring and Observability

Live systems must be observable in real time.

Monitor:

- Latency
- Order rejection rates
- Slippage
- Risk metrics
- Model prediction distribution

Example anomaly detection:

if abs(prediction) > historical_max_signal:

alert()

Unexpected behavior must trigger alerts.

No production system should run silently.

10. Logging and Audit Trail

Every action must be logged:

- Feature values
- Model predictions
- Orders submitted
- Fills received
- Risk overrides

Logs enable:

- Post-mortem analysis
- Compliance reporting

- Strategy attribution

Auditability is essential for institutional deployment.

11. Fault Tolerance and Redundancy

Live trading systems must handle:

- Network interruptions
- Exchange downtime
- Server failure
- Model crash

Mitigation:

- Redundant servers
- Heartbeat monitoring
- Automatic restart processes
- Backup execution logic

Example:

if heartbeat_missing:

switch_to_backup_server()

Design for failure, not perfection.

12. Kill Switch and Emergency Controls

A global emergency shutdown must exist.

Example:

if system_error_detected:

cancel_all_orders()

flatten_positions()

Kill switch must be independent from trading logic.

In extreme events, rapid response protects capital.

13. Deployment Workflow

Proper deployment includes:

- Research validation
- Paper trading
- Small capital live test
- Gradual scaling

Never move directly from backtest to full-scale deployment.

Staged rollout reduces systemic risk.

14. Version Control and Reproducibility

Every live model must be:

- Versioned
- Documented
- Reproducible

Store:

- Model parameters
- Training data snapshot
- Feature definitions

Reproducibility prevents debugging ambiguity.

15. Latency Considerations by Strategy Type

Latency requirements vary:

- **High-frequency trading** → microseconds matter
- **Daily strategies** → milliseconds sufficient

Architecture complexity must match strategy horizon.

Overengineering for slow strategies wastes resources.

Practical Architecture Checklist

Before going live:

- Modular system components defined.
- Risk engine independent from model.
- Execution engine validated in paper trading.

- Monitoring dashboards implemented.
- Logging and audit trails active.
- Kill switch tested.
- Redundancy and failover configured.

Live trading architecture is engineering discipline applied to financial risk.

Final Principle

In research, performance matters.

In production, reliability matters more.

A strong model inside a fragile architecture is a liability.

System architecture determines whether:

- Signals are applied correctly
- Risk is enforced consistently
- Failures are contained quickly

Live trading success depends as much on system design as on predictive power.

In autonomous trading systems, architecture is part of risk management.

14.2 Latency, Scalability, and Reliability

Once a trading agent moves from research to production, three engineering constraints become central:

- **Latency** – how fast the system reacts
- **Scalability** – how well it handles growth
- **Reliability** – how consistently it operates under stress

A profitable model deployed on unstable infrastructure will fail. Live trading performance is bounded by system engineering quality.

1. Latency: Reaction Time Matters

Latency is the time between:

- Market event
- Decision computation
- Order submission
- Order acknowledgment

For some strategies, latency determines profitability. For others, it is secondary but still important.

1.1 Latency Components

End-to-end latency includes:

- Market data transmission
- Data processing and feature computation
- Model inference
- Risk checks
- Order routing
- Exchange matching engine response

Total latency:

$$T_{total} = T_{data} + T_{compute} + T_{risk} + T_{routing}$$

Each component must be measured independently.

1.2 Matching Latency to Strategy Horizon

Latency requirements depend on signal half-life.

- **High-frequency strategies** → microseconds to milliseconds
- **Intraday strategies** → milliseconds to seconds
- **Daily strategies** → seconds acceptable

Over-optimizing latency for slow strategies increases complexity without benefit.

Architecture must match trading horizon.

1.3 Measuring Latency

Log timestamps at each stage:

t_data_received

t_features_ready

t_model_output

t_order_sent

t_ack_received

Compute stage-level latency.

Unexpected spikes often precede performance degradation.

1.4 Latency Control Techniques

- Co-locate servers near exchange
- Use event-driven architecture
- Pre-load models into memory
- Avoid blocking operations
- Use asynchronous order handling

Latency must be engineered, not assumed.

2. Scalability: Growing Without Breaking

Scalability means the system can handle:

- More assets

- More strategies
- Higher order volume
- Increased capital

Without redesign.

2.1 Horizontal vs Vertical Scaling

Vertical scaling:

- Stronger single machine

Horizontal scaling:

- Distributed components across multiple machines

For multi-asset systems, horizontal scaling is more robust.

Example:

- Separate feature computation per asset
- Parallel model inference

2.2 Distributed Architecture

Use modular services:

- Data service
- Feature service
- Model service
- Risk service
- Execution service

Communication through defined APIs or message queues.

This allows independent scaling of bottlenecks.

2.3 Throughput Testing

Simulate peak load:

- Burst market data
- High volatility periods

- Order spikes

Monitor:

- CPU utilization
- Memory usage
- Queue delays

If system lags during volatility spikes, risk exposure increases.

Scalability must be tested before stress conditions occur.

3. Reliability: Surviving Real-World Conditions

Reliability is the probability the system functions correctly under adverse conditions.

Markets do not wait for restarts.

3.1 Redundancy

Critical components require backup:

- Dual data feeds
- Backup execution gateway
- Failover servers

If primary fails:

switch_to_backup()

Redundancy reduces single points of failure.

3.2 State Persistence

Positions, orders, and cash balances must be persisted.

If system restarts, it must recover exact state.

Example:

load_state_from_database()

Stateless trading systems are unsafe.

3.3 Heartbeat Monitoring

Each service should emit periodic heartbeat.

If heartbeat missing:

trigger_alert()

Silent failure is unacceptable in live trading.

3.4 Graceful Degradation

If a component fails:

- Disable affected strategy
- Reduce exposure
- Maintain risk constraints

Example:

if model_service_unavailable:

set_position_to_zero()

Graceful degradation prevents cascading failure.

4. Risk Interaction with Infrastructure

Infrastructure failure directly increases financial risk.

Examples:

- **Delayed risk checks** → unintended leverage
- **Order acknowledgment loss** → duplicated orders
- **Stale data** → invalid decisions

System design must prioritize risk isolation.

Risk engine should operate even if model service is degraded.

5. Monitoring Latency and Reliability in Real Time

Dashboard metrics should include:

- End-to-end latency
- Order rejection rate
- Fill delay
- CPU/memory utilization
- Network packet loss

Automated alerts for threshold breaches.

Example:

if latency > max_latency:

reduce_strategy_activity()

Infrastructure health directly impacts trading decisions.

6. Stress Testing Infrastructure

Simulate:

- Market open surge
- Extreme volatility
- Exchange outage
- Network partition

Test:

- Recovery time
- Order reconciliation
- State consistency

Infrastructure stress testing is as important as financial stress testing.

7. Version Control and Deployment Discipline

Scalability and reliability depend on disciplined deployment.

Best practices:

- Staged rollout
- Canary deployments
- Rollback capability
- Immutable model artifacts

Never modify production code manually.

Controlled deployment prevents hidden instability.

8. Capacity Planning

As capital increases:

- Order size grows

- Market impact grows
- System load grows

Capacity planning includes:

- Hardware scaling
- Network bandwidth
- Database throughput

Failure to scale infrastructure often appears as performance decay.

9. Separation of Concerns

To improve reliability:

- Risk system independent from execution
- Monitoring independent from strategy
- Logging independent from inference

Coupled systems amplify failure.

Modular systems contain it.

Practical Engineering Checklist

Before scaling capital:

- Measure end-to-end latency.
- Perform load testing under peak conditions.
- Implement redundant data feeds.
- Ensure state persistence and recovery.
- Test failover and kill switch.
- Monitor infrastructure health continuously.
- Infrastructure must scale before capital does.

Final Principle

- Latency determines reactivity.
- Scalability determines growth capacity.
- Reliability determines survival.

A trading agent is only as strong as the system that runs it.

In live markets, infrastructure failures are financial events.

Engineering discipline is not separate from trading performance.

It is a core component of risk management and long-term profitability.

14.3 Monitoring, Logging, and Alerting

Once a trading system is live, you no longer control the environment. Markets move, data feeds fail, exchanges reject orders, and models drift. The only way to maintain control is continuous visibility.

Monitoring, logging, and alerting are not operational extras. They are real-time risk management tools.

A live AI trading system without observability is a liability.

This section defines what must be monitored, how to log correctly, and how to design effective alerts.

1. Monitoring: What Must Be Observed

Monitoring must cover three layers:

- Market & data integrity
- Strategy & model behavior
- Infrastructure health

All three interact.

1.1 Market & Data Monitoring

Track:

- Data feed latency
- Missing ticks
- Price anomalies
- Spread spikes
- Volume irregularities

Example validation:

if abs(price_change) > anomaly_threshold:

flag_data_issue()

Stale or corrupted data leads directly to bad decisions.

Always monitor data freshness:

if current_time - last_tick_time > max_delay:

suspend_trading()

Data integrity is the foundation of live trading.

1.2 Strategy & Model Monitoring

Track live performance metrics in real time:

- Rolling PnL
- Rolling Sharpe
- Drawdown
- Exposure
- Signal distribution

Example:

if abs(current_signal) > historical_max_signal:

trigger_alert()

Unexpected signal magnitude may indicate feature failure or model drift.

Also monitor:

- Prediction confidence
- Prediction distribution shift
- Model inference latency

If model output distribution changes significantly, investigate.

1.3 Risk Monitoring

Risk must be monitored continuously, not only at trade time.

Track:

- Gross exposure
- Net exposure
- Leverage
- Concentration
- Margin utilization

Example:

if gross_exposure > max_allowed:

reduce_positions()

Risk monitoring should operate independently from strategy logic.

Hard limits must trigger automatic action.

1.4 Execution Monitoring

Track:

- Slippage vs expected
- Fill rate
- Order rejection rate
- Partial fills
- Implementation shortfall

Example:

if average_slippage > slippage_threshold:

alert_execution_team()

Execution degradation often appears before strategy-level PnL decay.

1.5 Infrastructure Monitoring

Monitor:

- CPU usage
- Memory usage
- Network latency
- Service uptime
- Heartbeat signals

Example:

if service_heartbeat_missing:

failover()

Infrastructure health directly impacts trading risk.

2. Logging: Creating an Audit Trail

Logging is not debugging convenience. It is forensic evidence.

Every critical event must be logged:

- Feature values
- Model predictions
- Risk adjustments
- Orders submitted
- Order acknowledgments
- Fills received

Log structure example:

log_entry = {

"timestamp": timestamp,

"features": feature_snapshot,

"prediction": model_output,

"target_position": target,

"executed_position": actual,

}

Logs must be:

- Timestamped
- Immutable
- Persisted reliably
- Searchable

This enables:

- Attribution analysis
- Failure investigation
- Compliance reporting

If you cannot reconstruct a decision from logs, system governance is incomplete.

3. Alerting: Turning Monitoring into Action

Monitoring without alerting is passive observation.

Alerting must be:

- Specific
- Actionable
- Threshold-based
- Predefined

Avoid vague alerts such as "performance unusual."

Instead define:

- Drawdown exceeds X%
- Slippage exceeds Y basis points
- Latency exceeds Z milliseconds
- Data feed stale beyond N seconds

Example:

if rolling_drawdown < -0.10:

send_alert("Drawdown threshold breached")

ALERT THRESHOLDS SHOULD be defined before deployment.

4. Alert Severity Levels

Classify alerts:

- Informational
- Warning
- Critical

Informational:

- Slight latency increase

Warning:

- Model output distribution shift

Critical:

- Risk limit breached
- Data feed failure
- Execution disconnect

Critical alerts should trigger automatic protective action.

5. Avoiding Alert Fatigue

Too many alerts create complacency.

Best practices:

- Use meaningful thresholds
- Avoid redundant notifications
- Group related events
- Escalate only when necessary

Alerts must reflect material risk.

Noise reduces effectiveness.

6. Automated Protective Responses

Certain alerts should trigger automated responses.

Examples:

Drawdown breach:

reduce_leverage()

Data feed interruption:

pause_trading()

Execution failure:

cancel_all_orders()

Automation reduces reaction time and emotional decision-making.

7. Monitoring Model Drift

For ML agents, monitor feature and prediction distributions.

Example:

if feature_mean_live != feature_mean_train:

flag_distribution_shift()

Drift may indicate:

- Regime shift
- Data processing bug
- Structural market change

Model drift often precedes performance decay.

8. Real-Time Dashboards

Live dashboards should display:

- Current PnL
- Risk exposure
- Rolling performance metrics
- Latency
- Order status

Visualization improves situational awareness.

However, dashboards complement alerts. They do not replace them.

9. Post-Mortem Process

After incident:

- Extract logs
- Reconstruct decision sequence
- Identify root cause
- Document corrective action
- Update monitoring thresholds if needed

Every incident should improve system robustness.

Repeated failure without process improvement indicates governance weakness.

Practical Monitoring Checklist

Before live deployment:

- Data freshness checks implemented.

- Risk limits monitored independently.
- Execution metrics logged and tracked.
- Infrastructure health monitored.
- Alert thresholds defined and tested.
- Kill switch validated.
- Log retention and backup configured.
- Monitoring must be tested before going live.

Final Principle

- Models generate signals.
- Execution generates trades.
- Monitoring protects capital.

In live trading, failures are inevitable. Undetected failures are catastrophic.

Monitoring, logging, and alerting transform a trading agent from an experimental system into a controlled financial instrument.

Visibility is control.

In autonomous trading systems, observability is a core component of risk management and long-term survival.

Chapter 15: Governance, Compliance, and Ethics

Just because automation is possible doesn't mean it's harmless. I learned that responsible system design includes legal and ethical constraints—whether you like them or not.

This chapter covers regulatory considerations, explainability, and ethical responsibilities in automated trading.

15.1 Regulatory Landscape for Automated Trading

Automation does not remove responsibility.

When a trading agent places an order, the legal and regulatory responsibility remains with the firm or individual operating it. Regulatory compliance is not a legal afterthought. It is a system design constraint.

The regulatory landscape for automated trading varies by jurisdiction, asset class, and strategy type, but the core themes are consistent:

- Market integrity
- Risk control
- Transparency
- Accountability

This section focuses on practical regulatory considerations that directly affect system design.

1. Why Regulation Exists in Automated Trading

Automated trading introduces risks such as:

- Excessive order flow
- Market manipulation
- Systemic instability
- Flash crashes
- Operational failures

Regulators aim to:

- Maintain fair and orderly markets
- Prevent abusive practices
- Ensure firms manage operational risk

Designing trading agents without regulatory awareness creates legal and financial risk.

2. Algorithmic Trading vs High-Frequency Trading

Regulators often distinguish between:

- Algorithmic trading (automated decision and execution)

- High-frequency trading (low-latency, high message volume)

Even if a strategy is not high-frequency, it may still fall under algorithmic trading rules.

If your system:

- Automatically generates orders
- Makes independent execution decisions
- Operates without manual intervention

It is likely considered algorithmic trading under most frameworks.

3. Pre-Trade Risk Controls

Many regulatory regimes require pre-trade controls.

Common requirements:

- Maximum order size limits
- Price collars
- Fat-finger protection
- Maximum message rate

Example:

if order_size > max_order_limit:

reject_order()

PRE-TRADE RISK CHECKS must occur before order leaves the system.

These controls are not optional in regulated markets.

4. Market Abuse and Manipulation Risk

Automated systems must avoid patterns that resemble:

- Spoofing
- Layering
- Quote stuffing
- Wash trading

Even if unintentional, certain behaviors can trigger regulatory investigation.

Examples of risky behavior:

- Rapid order placement and cancellation without intent to execute
- Artificially influencing price levels

Execution logic must be designed to avoid manipulative patterns.

Intent is difficult to prove. Behavior matters more.

5. Audit Trail and Record-Keeping

Regulators often require:

- Full order lifecycle records
- Timestamped logs
- Model documentation
- Change management records

Your system must log:

- Decision inputs
- Model outputs
- Risk checks applied
- Orders submitted
- Execution results

If you cannot reconstruct why a trade occurred, compliance exposure increases.

Logging architecture is part of regulatory compliance.

6. Kill Switch and Circuit Breakers

Many jurisdictions require:

- Emergency kill switch
- Automatic shutdown mechanisms
- Self-monitoring systems

Example:

if abnormal_activity_detected:

cancel_all_orders()

disable_trading()

Kill switch must be:

- Independent from strategy logic
- Manually accessible
- Rapidly executable

Operational safeguards are regulatory expectations.

7. Model Governance and Change Control

For AI-driven systems, regulators increasingly focus on:

- Model transparency
- Version control
- Testing documentation
- Approval workflows

Best practices:

- Document model training process
- Record parameter changes
- Maintain version history
- Use staged deployment

Uncontrolled model updates increase regulatory risk.

8. Market Access Controls

If trading through broker or direct market access (DMA):

You may be required to implement:

- Credit checks
- Exposure limits
- Real-time margin monitoring

Example:

if margin_usage > threshold:

block_new_orders()

Market access rules aim to prevent destabilizing order flow.

9. Cross-Border Considerations

Different jurisdictions impose different rules.

Key differences may include:

- Order-to-trade ratio limits
- Reporting obligations
- Short-selling restrictions
- Data retention requirements

If trading globally, system must adapt compliance controls per venue.

Regulatory fragmentation increases complexity.

10. Surveillance and Reporting

Firms may be required to:

- Submit transaction reports
- Report suspicious activity
- Maintain communication logs

Automated reporting systems should be integrated into infrastructure.

Manual reporting is error-prone.

11. Ethical vs Legal Compliance

Legal compliance defines minimum requirement.

Ethical design goes further:

- Avoid excessive market impact
- Avoid exploiting fragile liquidity
- Design stable algorithms

Just because behavior is legal does not mean it is sustainable.

Regulatory scrutiny increases during market stress.

12. Governance Framework for Automated Trading

A professional automated trading governance structure includes:

- Model validation before deployment
- Independent risk oversight
- Documented testing procedures
- Deployment approval process
- Ongoing monitoring and audit

Governance must be institutionalized, not informal.

13. Integrating Compliance into System Design

Compliance should be embedded directly into architecture.

Examples:

- Pre-trade risk module
- Real-time exposure monitoring
- Structured logging
- Immutable audit storage
- Automated regulatory reporting

Compliance should not depend on manual oversight alone.

Automation requires automated compliance.

Practical Regulatory Checklist

Before going live:

- Implement pre-trade risk controls.
- Define maximum order and exposure limits.
- Ensure full audit logging.
- Implement kill switch and emergency controls.
- Document model development and testing.
- Validate order-to-trade behavior.
- Confirm jurisdiction-specific requirements.

Ignoring regulation is not a technical risk. It is a business risk.

Final Principle

Automated trading increases speed and scale.

Regulation ensures stability and accountability.

A well-designed AI trading system must operate within:

- Legal constraints
- Risk boundaries
- Ethical considerations

Compliance is not separate from system design.

It is a structural requirement for sustainable operation in regulated financial markets.

Autonomy does not remove responsibility.

It increases it.

15.2 Model Transparency and Explainability

As trading systems become more autonomous and model complexity increases, transparency becomes harder—and more necessary.

A profitable model that cannot be explained is:

- Difficult to debug
- Hard to govern
- Risky to scale
- Vulnerable to regulatory scrutiny

Explainability is not about making deep learning simple. It is about making decisions auditable and accountable.

This section focuses on practical approaches to model transparency in AI-driven trading systems.

1. Why Explainability Matters

Explainability serves four core purposes:

- Risk management
- Regulatory compliance
- Debugging and performance attribution
- Investor communication

If a model generates a large position, you must answer:

- What signals drove the decision?
- Was it consistent with historical behavior?
- Was risk control applied correctly?

Opaque systems increase operational risk.

2. Levels of Model Transparency

Transparency exists at different levels.

2.1 Structural Transparency

Understanding:

- Model architecture
- Inputs
- Outputs
- Training process

Example documentation:

- Feature definitions
- Target variable
- Training window
- Hyperparameters

Structural clarity is the minimum requirement.

2.2 Feature-Level Transparency

Which features influence decisions?

For linear models:

*contribution = feature_value * coefficient*

Coefficients directly show direction and magnitude of influence.

If a volatility feature suddenly dominates decisions, this is observable.

2.3 Local Decision Explainability

Explain a single prediction.

- For tree-based models and neural networks, use feature attribution techniques.

Example (conceptual):

shap_values = explainer.shap_values(feature_vector)

SHAP values estimate contribution of each feature to a specific prediction.

Local explanations answer:

- Why did the model generate this specific signal now?

This is essential during unusual trades.

2.4 Global Model Behavior

Assess overall feature importance across dataset.

Questions:

- Which features consistently drive predictions?
- Has importance shifted over time?

If model behavior changes significantly without retraining, investigate drift.

3. Explainability in Reinforcement Learning

RL agents are harder to interpret because they optimize policy rather than predict outcomes.

Approaches include:

- Policy sensitivity analysis
- State-action value inspection
- Action distribution monitoring

Example:

action_distribution = policy(state_batch)

MONITOR:

- Distribution stability
- Sudden behavior changes
- Risk-taking patterns

RL systems require stronger monitoring discipline.

4. Detecting Model Drift Through Transparency

Explainability tools help detect:

- Feature distribution shifts
- Changing feature importance
- Prediction bias

Example:

If live feature mean deviates from training mean:

if abs(live_mean - train_mean) > threshold:

alert()

Drift detection supports proactive maintenance.

5. Transparency vs Complexity Trade-Off

Complex models:

- May capture nonlinear patterns
- Reduce interpretability

Simple models:

- Easier to explain
- More stable
- Often more robust

In many financial applications, moderate complexity outperforms extreme model depth.

Explainability often correlates with robustness.

6. Documentation and Version Control

Transparency includes documentation.

For each deployed model, record:

- Training dataset snapshot
- Feature list
- Hyperparameters
- Validation metrics
- Deployment date

Version example:

model_version = "v2.3.1"

If performance degrades, you must know which version is active.

Reproducibility is part of explainability.

7. Real-Time Decision Logging

For each trade decision, log:

- Feature values
- Model prediction

- Confidence score
- Risk adjustments
- Final executed size

Example:

decision_log = {

"timestamp": t,

"features": feature_snapshot,

"prediction": y_hat,

"risk_adjusted_position": final_position

}

This enables post-trade analysis and audit review.

8. Explainability for Stakeholders

Investors and risk managers require understandable reasoning.

Communicate:

- Strategy logic in plain language
- Risk controls embedded in system
- Situations where model performs poorly

Avoid overstating certainty.

Transparency builds credibility.

9. Regulatory Expectations

In regulated markets, explainability requirements may include:

- Model governance documentation
- Risk validation procedures
- Decision traceability
- Independent review process

Black-box models without documentation increase compliance risk.

Transparency reduces legal and operational exposure.

10. Practical Explainability Framework

Before deployment:

- Document feature definitions.
- Log model coefficients or importance scores.
- Implement local explanation tools for predictions.
- Monitor feature drift.
- Track prediction distribution stability.
- Maintain version-controlled model registry.

Transparency must be operational, not theoretical.

11. Limits of Explainability

Not all models can be perfectly explained.

However:

- You must understand dominant drivers.
- You must detect abnormal behavior.
- You must reconstruct decisions after the fact.

Complete interpretability is unrealistic.

Structured accountability is not.

Final Principle

Autonomous trading systems increase decision speed and complexity.

Transparency ensures control remains with the operator.

Explainability:

- Reduces model risk
- Supports regulatory compliance
- Improves debugging
- Strengthens stakeholder trust

A model that cannot be explained cannot be governed.

In AI-driven trading, transparency is not a philosophical concern.

It is a structural requirement for responsible automation.

15.3 Ethical Considerations in Autonomous Markets

Autonomous trading systems operate at speed, scale, and opacity that exceed human capability. That power creates responsibility.

Ethics in automated trading is not abstract philosophy. It directly affects:

- Market stability
- Fair access to liquidity
- Systemic risk
- Public trust in financial markets

An AI trading agent may optimize profit, but the firm deploying it must define acceptable boundaries.

This section focuses on practical ethical considerations in designing and operating autonomous trading systems.

1. Profit Maximization vs Market Integrity

A trading agent optimized purely for return may:

- Exploit temporary liquidity gaps
- Increase volatility during stress
- Amplify feedback loops

Ethical design requires balancing:

- Profit objectives
- Market stability
- Responsible participation

Just because a behavior is profitable does not mean it is sustainable.

Short-term profit at the cost of systemic instability damages long-term market structure.

2. Market Manipulation Risks

Autonomous systems can unintentionally generate patterns that resemble:

- Spoofing
- Layering

- Momentum ignition
- Quote stuffing

Even if the model has no intent to manipulate, behavior matters.

Ethical safeguards include:

- Limiting excessive order cancellations
- Avoiding artificial order book pressure
- Preventing rapid placement and withdrawal patterns

Execution policies must be constrained to avoid destabilizing behavior.

3. Liquidity Responsibility

Large automated systems influence market liquidity.

Questions to consider:

- Does the strategy withdraw liquidity during stress?
- Does it exacerbate volatility spikes?
- Does it concentrate risk in fragile instruments?

Some strategies may appear profitable because they extract liquidity during panic conditions.

Ethical system design includes stress-aware controls:

if market_volatility > threshold:

reduce_aggressiveness()

Participation should not intentionally amplify disorder.

4. Fair Access and Technological Advantage

Low-latency trading creates asymmetry.

While speed advantage is legal in many markets, ethical considerations include:

- Avoiding exploitation of microstructural weaknesses
- Avoiding strategies that depend on predictable slower participants
- Market ecosystems rely on fairness perceptions.

Excessive exploitation may invite regulatory reaction and structural reform.

5. Systemic Risk Amplification

Highly correlated AI systems can create:

- Herding behavior
- Liquidity cascades
- Flash crashes

If many agents react to similar signals simultaneously, market instability increases.

Ethical design includes:

- Position limits
- Volatility scaling
- Circuit breakers

Self-restraint reduces systemic risk contribution.

6. Transparency to Stakeholders

Ethical trading requires transparency to:

- Investors
- Risk managers
- Regulators

Stakeholders should understand:

- Strategy objectives
- Risk limits
- Failure scenarios

Opaque systems increase reputational and governance risk.

Transparency builds trust.

7. Responsible Use of Alternative Data

AI systems may use:

- News sentiment
- Social media
- Behavioral indicators

Ethical considerations include:

- Data privacy
- Legality of data sources
- Avoiding misuse of non-public information

Using improperly sourced data creates legal and ethical violations.

Data governance is part of ethical system design.

8. Model Bias and Feedback Effects

Autonomous trading models may learn patterns that:

- Reinforce volatility
- Exploit fragile participants
- React aggressively to price dislocations

Unconstrained reinforcement learning can discover destabilizing strategies.

Ethical safeguards include:

- Reward penalties for excessive volatility impact
- Explicit constraints on leverage
- Controlled exploration

Optimization must occur within boundaries.

9. Crisis Behavior and Kill Switch Responsibility

During extreme market events, autonomous systems may:

- Accelerate losses
- Increase order flow instability

Ethical system design requires:

- Emergency shutdown procedures
- Human oversight capability
- Defined escalation protocols

Responsibility does not disappear because a model made the decision.

Humans remain accountable.

10. Long-Term Sustainability vs Short-Term Exploitation

Some strategies exploit:

- Temporary inefficiencies
- Structural imbalances
- Regulatory gaps

Sustainable trading focuses on:

- Genuine information advantage
- Risk-managed participation
- Stability over extraction

Long-term viability depends on responsible engagement with markets.

11. Governance and Oversight

Ethical autonomous trading requires governance structure:

- Independent risk oversight
- Model validation committees
- Clear accountability lines
- Periodic review of strategy impact

Governance reduces ethical drift.

Profit pressure can erode discipline without formal oversight.

12. Aligning Incentives

Compensation structures influence behavior.

If incentives reward:

- Short-term return only

Risk-taking may increase beyond acceptable bounds.

Balanced evaluation should include:

- Risk-adjusted performance

- Compliance adherence
- Operational stability

Ethics must align with incentives.

Practical Ethical Design Checklist

Before deploying autonomous trading systems:

- Define acceptable behavior boundaries.
- Enforce risk limits and leverage constraints.
- Monitor market impact during stress.
- Implement emergency controls.
- Ensure data usage is compliant and ethical.
- Maintain clear accountability for decisions.
- Periodically review systemic impact.

Ethics must be embedded in architecture and governance, not assumed.

Final Principle

Autonomous trading increases speed and scale of decision-making.

With autonomy comes amplified responsibility.

Ethical system design:

- Protects market integrity
- Reduces systemic risk
- Supports regulatory compliance
- Preserves long-term sustainability

AI trading agents operate in shared markets.

Maximizing profit while preserving stability is not optional.

It is the condition for continued participation in autonomous financial systems.

Chapter 16: Maintaining and Evolving Trading Agents

Markets evolve faster than most people expect. Agents that don't adapt quietly decay. I've learned that maintenance is not a failure—it's the job.

This chapter focuses on retraining, adaptation, regime shifts, and long-term agent lifecycle management.

16.1 Continuous Learning and Model Retraining

Markets evolve. Models do not—unless you update them.

A model trained on historical data reflects past structure. If that structure shifts, performance degrades. Continuous learning is not optional in live trading systems. It is part of lifecycle management.

However, retraining blindly can be as dangerous as not retraining at all.

This section defines how to design disciplined, controlled model updating frameworks.

1. Why Models Need Retraining

Financial markets are:

- Non-stationary
- Regime-dependent
- Influenced by changing participant behavior

Feature relationships shift over time:

- Momentum strength varies
- Volatility structure evolves
- Liquidity patterns change

If you freeze a model indefinitely, decay is inevitable.

But retraining must be governed by structure, not reaction to short-term noise.

2. Types of Continuous Learning

There are three main approaches:

- Periodic retraining
- Rolling window retraining
- Online learning

Each has trade-offs.

3. Periodic Retraining

Retrain model at fixed intervals:

- Monthly
- Quarterly
- Annually

Example:

if current_date >= retrain_date:

retrain_model(

- Predictable
- Controlled
- Easy to audit

Disadvantages:

- May miss rapid regime shifts
- May retrain unnecessarily during stable periods

Most institutional systems start here.

4. Rolling Window Retraining

Use most recent N observations for training.

Example:

train_data = data[-rolling_window:]

model.fit(train_data)

Benefits:

- Emphasizes recent market structure
- Gradually removes stale data

Risk:

- **Window too short** → noisy model
- **Window too long** → slow adaptation

Selecting appropriate window length requires validation.

5. Online Learning

Model updates incrementally as new data arrives.

Example (conceptual):

model.partial_fit(new_observation)

Advantages:

- Fast adaptation
- Continuous learning

Risks:

- Drift from noise
- Overreaction to recent volatility
- Harder reproducibility

Online learning requires strict monitoring and constraints.

6. Retraining Triggers

Instead of fixed schedule, use performance-based triggers.

Examples:

if rolling_sharpe < threshold:

initiate_retraining()

Or:

if prediction_error_mean > drift_limit:

retrain()

Triggers must be predefined.

Reactive retraining without rules introduces bias.

7. Preventing Overfitting During Retraining

Common mistake:

- Retrain aggressively after drawdown.
- This often fits recent noise rather than structural change.

Safeguards:

- Minimum training window length

- Minimum data requirement
- Out-of-sample validation after retraining
- Parameter stability checks

Retraining must include validation step before redeployment.

8. Walk-Forward Retraining Framework

Structured retraining workflow:

- Train on rolling window
- Validate on recent holdout
- Compare performance to current live model
- Deploy only if improvement statistically meaningful

Example evaluation:

if new_model_sharpe > current_model_sharpe + margin:

deploy_new_model()

Deployment must be evidence-based.

9. Model Versioning and Auditability

Every retrained model must be:

- Versioned
- Logged
- Reproducible

Store:

- Training dataset snapshot
- Feature definitions
- Hyperparameters
- Evaluation metrics

Example:

model_version = "v3.2.0"

Without version control, diagnosing live issues becomes impossible.

10. Feature Stability Monitoring

Before retraining, check feature drift.

Example:

if abs(live_feature_mean - training_mean) > threshold:

flag_feature_shift()

Sometimes feature recalibration is sufficient.

Not all performance decline requires model architecture change.

11. Regime-Aware Retraining

Instead of uniform retraining, adapt model per regime.

Example:

- Train separate models for high-vol and low-vol regimes
- Update only active regime model
- This reduces unnecessary churn.

Adaptive retraining must maintain structural consistency.

12. Safeguards Against Catastrophic Updates

Never immediately replace live model without testing.

Deployment sequence:

- Paper trade new model
- Run shadow mode alongside live model
- Compare signals
- Gradually shift capital

Example:

allocation_new = 0.2

allocation_old = 0.8

Gradual transition reduces risk.

13. Monitoring Post-Retraining Behavior

After deployment:

- Monitor signal distribution
- Monitor turnover
- Monitor risk exposure
- Compare realized vs expected return

If new model behaves unexpectedly, revert.

Rollback capability is mandatory.

14. When Not to Retrain

Avoid retraining when:

- Short-term drawdown within historical bounds
- No feature drift observed
- Regime consistent with training data

Over-retraining increases instability.

Sometimes patience is better than intervention.

Practical Continuous Learning Checklist

- Define retraining frequency or triggers.
- Use rolling or expanding window appropriately.
- Validate before deployment.
- Version-control all models.
- Monitor feature drift.
- Test new models in shadow mode.
- Maintain rollback capability.

Retraining is controlled adaptation, not reactive experimentation.

Final Principle

Markets evolve.

Models must adapt—but with discipline.

Continuous learning improves durability only when governed by:

- Structured validation

- Version control
- Risk oversight
- Conservative deployment

Uncontrolled retraining introduces more instability than it solves.

In AI-driven trading, adaptation must be systematic, auditable, and aligned with long-term robustness.

Continuous learning is part of lifecycle management—not an emergency response.

16.2 Handling Market Regime Shifts

Most strategies fail not because the model is poorly designed, but because the market environment changes.

A regime shift is not normal volatility. It is a structural change in behavior:

- Volatility regime transitions
- Correlation breakdowns
- Liquidity collapse
- Policy-driven market shifts
- Participant behavior changes

Handling regime shifts requires preparation before they occur.

This section outlines practical frameworks for identifying, managing, and surviving regime changes.

1. What Defines a Regime Shift?

A regime shift typically involves changes in:

- Volatility level
- Correlation structure
- Trend persistence
- Liquidity depth
- Return distribution shape

Examples:

- Transition from low-vol trending to high-vol mean-reverting
- Crisis-induced liquidity withdrawal
- Central bank intervention altering macro dynamics

Regime shifts invalidate historical assumptions embedded in models.

2. Early Detection Signals

Regime shifts rarely occur without warning.

Monitor:

2.1 Volatility Expansion

```
vol_short = returns.rolling(20).std()
vol_long = returns.rolling(100).std()
if vol_short > 1.5 * vol_long:
flag_volatility_shift()
```

Sustained volatility spikes often indicate structural transition.

2.2 Correlation Spike

In multi-asset portfolios:

```
avg_corr = returns_df.rolling(60).corr().mean()
```

If cross-asset correlation increases sharply, diversification assumptions break down.

2.3 Signal Decay

Declining rolling information coefficient:

```
rolling_ic = signal.rolling(252).corr(future_return)
```

Persistent IC collapse suggests structural shift.

3. Predefined Defensive Adjustments

Do not improvise during regime shifts.

Predefine defensive actions.

Examples:

- Reduce leverage
- Increase cash allocation
- Tighten position limits
- Slow execution aggressiveness

Example:

```
if regime_flag:
leverage *= 0.5
```

Automatic scaling reduces emotional decision-making.

4. Volatility-Based Risk Scaling

Volatility targeting is one of the most effective regime response mechanisms.

target_vol = 0.12

position_size = target_vol / current_vol

As volatility rises, exposure falls.

This dampens drawdowns during structural transitions.

5. Strategy Diversification Across Regimes

Design portfolio to include strategies that perform differently across environments:

- Momentum
- Mean reversion
- Volatility breakout
- Defensive allocation

When one regime weakens a strategy, others may stabilize portfolio.

Regime diversification reduces dependence on single assumption.

6. Adaptive Weighting

Shift allocation dynamically based on detected regime.

Example:

if high_vol_regime:

weight_momentum = 0.6

weight_mean_rev = 0.4

else:

weight_momentum = 0.3

weight_mean_rev = 0.7

Weight adjustments should be gradual, not abrupt.

Hard switching increases turnover and instability.

7. Parameter Recalibration

Sometimes regime shift requires recalibration.

Examples:

- Shorter lookback windows in volatile markets
- Wider thresholds in noisy conditions

However, recalibration must be validated, not reactive.

Test new parameters in controlled environment before deployment.

8. Stress Testing Against Historical Regimes

Before deployment, simulate past regime transitions:

- Financial crisis periods
- Volatility spikes
- Liquidity crunches

If strategy fails catastrophically in historical regime transitions, it is vulnerable.

Stress testing prepares system for plausible future events.

9. Gradual De-Risking Framework

Instead of binary shutdown:

- Reduce allocation by fixed percentage.
- Monitor stabilization.
- Reassess performance metrics.

Example:

if rolling_sharpe < threshold:

*allocation *= 0.7*

Gradual response prevents overreaction to noise.

10. Distinguishing Noise from Structural Change

Short-term losses do not always indicate regime shift.

Differentiate between:

- Normal drawdown
- Statistical anomaly
- Structural break

Compare live metrics to historical Monte Carlo ranges.

If performance remains within expected distribution, patience may be appropriate.

11. Reinforcement Learning and Regime Shifts

RL systems can adapt to regime changes if state representation includes:

- Volatility indicators
- Correlation metrics
- Drawdown state

However, RL agents may struggle during rare extreme events.

Hard-coded constraints must override learned behavior.

12. Human Oversight During Structural Events

Fully autonomous systems still require oversight.

During:

- Policy shocks
- Geopolitical crises
- Exchange halts

Human judgment may temporarily override automated systems.

Autonomy does not eliminate governance.

13. Post-Shift Analysis

After regime transition stabilizes:

- Review strategy performance drivers.
- Evaluate feature relevance changes.
- Update training dataset if necessary.
- Adjust risk assumptions.

Regime shifts are learning opportunities.

Structured review improves resilience.

Practical Regime Shift Response Checklist

- Monitor volatility and correlation continuously.
- Define defensive scaling rules in advance.

- Stress-test extreme historical environments.
- Diversify across strategy types.
- Avoid abrupt full shutdown unless systemic failure occurs.
- Review performance after transition.

Preparedness reduces panic.

Final Principle

Market regime shifts are inevitable.

The objective is not to predict every shift perfectly.

It is to design systems that:

- Detect structural changes early
- Reduce risk automatically
- Maintain stability through transitions
- Recover intelligently afterward

Adaptive systems survive longer than static systems.

In autonomous trading, resilience to regime shifts defines long-term durability.

16.3 Debugging and Improving Live Agents

A trading agent in production will eventually behave unexpectedly.

Performance drifts. Signals look different. Slippage increases. Risk spikes without clear explanation.

Debugging live agents is not the same as debugging research code. In live systems, errors carry financial consequences. Improvements must be controlled, auditable, and risk-aware.

This section outlines a structured framework for diagnosing and improving live trading agents.

1. First Principle: Separate Symptoms from Causes

When performance deteriorates, do not immediately retrain.

Common surface symptoms:

- Negative rolling Sharpe
- Increased drawdown
- Higher turnover
- Execution slippage increase

These are symptoms. Root causes may include:

- Model decay
- Feature drift
- Regime shift
- Cost structure change
- Infrastructure latency

Effective debugging begins with classification.

2. Step 1: Verify Data Integrity

Before analyzing the model, confirm that inputs are correct.

Check:

- Missing data
- Timestamp misalignment

- Corporate action adjustments
- Unexpected feature scaling changes

Example:

if live_feature_mean != training_feature_mean:

flag_feature_shift()

Data bugs are more common than model failure.

Never assume the model is wrong before validating inputs.

3. Step 2: Compare Live vs Backtest Assumptions

Differences often emerge between research and production.

Check:

- Slippage assumptions
- Commission changes
- Latency increases
- Liquidity conditions

Example:

*if realized_slippage > modeled_slippage * 1.5:*

investigate_execution()

Execution drift may explain most performance decay.

4. Step 3: Analyze Prediction Drift

Compare predicted returns to realized returns.

prediction_error = predicted - realized

rolling_bias = prediction_error.rolling(100).mean()

Persistent bias suggests:

- Regime shift
- Feature miscalibration
- Model degradation

If predictions remain stable but returns deteriorate, problem may lie in execution or allocation.

5. Step 4: Attribution Decomposition

Decompose performance:

- Signal return
- Allocation effect
- Execution effect
- Factor exposure

If theoretical signal return remains strong but realized return declines, execution or cost layer is failing.

If both degrade, model decay is likely.

6. Step 5: Check Risk Controls

Ensure risk layer is functioning properly.

Monitor:

- Leverage limits
- Concentration exposure
- Drawdown scaling

Example:

if gross_exposure > max_allowed:

reduce_positions()

If risk constraints are misapplied, unexpected drawdowns occur.

Sometimes the bug is not in the model but in risk override logic.

7. Common Live Failure Modes

7.1 Feature Pipeline Drift

Feature calculation differs between research and production.

Symptom:

- Signal distribution shifts abruptly.

7.2 Regime Structural Change

Market behavior shifts, degrading signal predictive power.

Symptom:

- Rolling IC collapses.

7.3 Cost Model Mismatch

Real transaction costs exceed modeled assumptions.

Symptom:

- High turnover but low net profitability.

7.4 Infrastructure Latency

Delayed execution erodes short-horizon edge.

Symptom:

- Implementation shortfall increases.

7.5 Parameter Overfitting

Model trained too specifically to historical period.

Symptom:

- Performance stable in backtest, unstable live.

8. Controlled Improvement Process

Never modify live system without structured evaluation.

Improvement workflow:

- Reproduce issue in research environment.
- Diagnose root cause.
- Develop modified version offline.
- Validate on rolling out-of-sample data.
- Paper trade new version.
- Deploy gradually with partial capital.

Example allocation shift:

new_model_weight = 0.3

old_model_weight = 0.7

Gradual deployment reduces transition risk.

9. Shadow Mode Testing

Run new model in parallel without executing trades.

Compare:

- Signal correlation
- Position differences
- Hypothetical PnL

Shadow testing reveals unintended behavior before capital exposure.

10. Logging for Debugging

Comprehensive logging enables reconstruction.

Log:

- Feature values
- Model output
- Risk adjustments
- Orders sent
- Execution results

Example:

log_decision(timestamp, features, prediction, position)

Without detailed logs, root cause analysis becomes guesswork.

11. Performance Threshold Triggers

Predefine triggers for investigation.

Example:

if rolling_sharpe < 0 for 60 days:

initiate_review()

Triggers reduce emotional reaction to short-term noise.

Consistent discipline prevents over-adjustment.

12. Avoiding Overreaction

Not every drawdown requires intervention.

Compare current drawdown to historical distribution via Monte Carlo.

If within expected range, patience may be warranted.

Frequent model changes increase instability.

13. Continuous Improvement Framework

Periodic review cycle:

- Monthly performance review
- Quarterly feature stability analysis
- Semiannual architecture audit
- Annual strategy redesign evaluation

Improvement must be structured and documented.

14. Human Oversight and Accountability

Autonomous agents operate automatically, but oversight remains human responsibility.

Define:

- Who approves changes
- Who monitors risk
- Who triggers shutdown

Clear accountability reduces operational ambiguity.

Practical Debugging Checklist

When performance declines:

- Validate data integrity.
- Compare live costs to modeled costs.
- Analyze prediction error drift.
- Decompose signal vs execution effects.
- Review risk constraint enforcement.
- Test modified version offline.
- Deploy gradually.

Structured debugging protects capital.

Final Principle

Live agents will degrade.

The objective is not perfection. It is controlled adaptation.

Debugging live systems requires:

- Discipline
- Logging
- Attribution
- Version control
- Gradual improvement

Emotional reaction to short-term performance destroys robustness.

In AI-driven trading, improvement must be systematic, evidence-based, and risk-aware.

Stability first. Optimization second.

Chapter 17: Future Directions in AI Trading

The future is not fully autonomous, fully human, or fully predictable. It's collaborative, adaptive, and constantly changing. The real edge will belong to those who design systems that evolve responsibly.

This chapter explores emerging trends in AI trading, multi-agent systems, self-improving models, and the evolving role of human oversight.

17.1 Self-Improving and Meta-Learning Agents

Traditional trading models learn from historical data and remain fixed until retrained.

Self-improving and meta-learning agents go further. They attempt to:

- Adapt to new environments
- Learn how to learn
- Adjust internal parameters dynamically
- Improve decision policies over time

The goal is not constant retraining, but structural adaptability.

However, self-improvement must be constrained. Uncontrolled adaptation introduces instability.

This section outlines practical architectures for building self-improving trading agents responsibly.

1. What Is a Self-Improving Agent?

A self-improving agent modifies some part of its decision process based on new experience.

This may include:

- Updating model weights
- Adjusting feature importance
- Modifying signal thresholds
- Updating capital allocation rules

Key distinction:

- Traditional retraining = manual update.
- Self-improvement = automated adaptive update.

2. Meta-Learning: Learning How to Adapt

Meta-learning focuses on learning adaptation rules rather than static predictions.

Instead of learning:

$$f(x) \to y$$

The system learns:

$$g(\text{model, environment}) \rightarrow \text{updated model}$$

In practice, this may mean:

- Learning optimal retraining frequency
- Learning adaptive weighting across strategies
- Learning regime-switching thresholds

Meta-learning operates one level above base models.

3. Adaptive Model Weighting

Simplest form of meta-learning:

- Adjust model weights based on recent performance.

Example:

weight_i = rolling_sharpe_i / sum(abs(rolling_sharpe))

Weights shift gradually toward better-performing models.

Advantages:

- Simple
- Transparent
- Controlled

This is often more robust than fully online retraining.

4. Regime-Conditioned Model Selection

Meta-layer selects which model to activate.

Example:

if volatility_regime == "high":

use_model_A()

else:

use_model_B()

Meta-agent does not predict returns directly. It predicts which strategy is appropriate.

This separation reduces instability.

5. Online Parameter Adaptation

Models may update parameters incrementally:

model.partial_fit(new_data)

Safeguards required:

- Learning rate limits
- Minimum data thresholds
- Performance-based validation

Unbounded online learning risks overfitting to recent noise.

6. Reinforcement Learning for Meta-Control

A higher-level RL agent can control:

- Capital allocation
- Risk scaling
- Execution aggressiveness

Example state:

state = {

"rolling_sharpe": sharpe,

"drawdown": drawdown,

"volatility": vol

}

Meta-agent outputs:

allocation_adjustment = meta_policy(state)

Meta-control layer adapts slower than signal layer.

This separation improves stability.

7. Performance-Triggered Retraining

Meta-layer decides when retraining occurs.

Example:

```
if rolling_ic < threshold:
retrain_flag = True
```

Rather than retraining on schedule, system retrains based on structural indicators.

This reduces unnecessary updates.

8. Safeguards for Self-Improving Systems

Autonomous improvement requires strict guardrails:

- Version control for each update
- Shadow testing before activation
- Performance comparison with baseline
- Rollback capability

Example:

```
if new_model_performance < baseline:
revert_to_previous_version()
```

Self-improvement without rollback is unacceptable.

9. Preventing Instability

Self-modifying systems risk:

- Oscillatory behavior
- Excessive turnover
- Parameter drift
- Risk amplification

Mitigation:

- Limit update frequency
- Cap allocation changes
- Apply smoothing

Example:

```
new_weight = 0.9 * old_weight + 0.1 * suggested_weight
```

Stability > speed of adaptation.

10. Meta-Learning with Regime Awareness

Advanced approach:

- Meta-model predicts regime transition probability.

Then adjusts:

- Risk exposure
- Strategy mix
- Feature emphasis

This combines regime detection with adaptive control.

However, complexity must be justified by measurable improvement.

11. Monitoring Self-Improving Agents

Additional monitoring required:

- Frequency of updates
- Magnitude of parameter changes
- Stability of allocations
- Drift from baseline performance

Self-improving systems must remain observable and interpretable.

12. When Self-Improvement Adds Value

Self-improving systems are most useful when:

- Market structure changes gradually
- Multiple models with complementary strengths exist
- Allocation decisions dominate performance

Less useful when:

- Edge is narrow and fragile
- Data volume insufficient
- Execution cost dominates performance

Complexity must be justified by measurable benefit.

13. Risk Governance in Adaptive Systems

Governance must include:

- Approval thresholds for structural change
- Documentation of update logic
- Independent risk oversight

Even autonomous systems require human accountability.

Adaptation should not bypass governance.

Practical Implementation Roadmap

- Start with static baseline model.
- Add performance-based weighting layer.
- Introduce regime-aware switching.
- Gradually test limited online adaptation.
- Maintain rollback and version history.
- Build adaptation incrementally.

Final Principle

Markets evolve.

Self-improving and meta-learning agents aim to evolve with them.

However, adaptability without discipline becomes instability.

Effective self-improvement requires:

- Structured update rules
- Risk constraints
- Monitoring and rollback
- Controlled deployment

In autonomous trading systems, the best adaptive agents are those that improve gradually, transparently, and within strict risk boundaries.

Self-improvement must enhance robustness, not amplify fragility.

17.2 Integration with Decentralized and Global Markets

AI trading agents are no longer confined to a single exchange or region. Capital flows across:

- Equities
- Futures
- FX
- Commodities
- Crypto assets
- Tokenized instruments
- Decentralized finance (DeFi) protocols

Future-ready agents must operate across fragmented, global, and decentralized market structures.

Integration introduces opportunity—but also complexity.

This section outlines practical design considerations for deploying AI trading agents across global and decentralized ecosystems.

1. Structural Differences Across Markets

Before integration, understand structural variation:

Market Type	Key Characteristics
Equities	Centralized exchanges, regulated clearing
Futures	Standardized contracts, leverage
FX	OTC, fragmented liquidity
Crypto	24/7 trading, exchange fragmentation
DeFi	Smart contract-based execution

Agents must adapt to structural constraints, not assume uniform behavior.

2. Global Market Integration

2.1 Multi-Time-Zone Operation

Global trading requires:

- Continuous monitoring
- Asynchronous scheduling
- Region-specific holiday calendars

Example:

if exchange_open(region):

activate_strategy(region)

Time-zone awareness prevents unintended exposure.

2.2 Currency Risk Management

Cross-border trading introduces FX exposure.

Even if strategy targets foreign equities, currency risk must be managed.

Example:

net_fx_exposure = foreign_asset_value - fx_hedge_position

Unmanaged currency drift distorts performance attribution.

2.3 Regulatory Fragmentation

Each jurisdiction imposes unique constraints.

Agents must incorporate:

- Venue-specific order rules
- Reporting obligations
- Leverage limits

Architecture must support rule-based configuration per region.

3. Crypto and 24/7 Markets

Crypto markets introduce structural changes:

- No closing hours
- Continuous liquidity cycles
- Exchange-specific order books

- Custody risks

Agents must handle:

- Overnight risk continuously
- Exchange reliability differences
- Cross-exchange arbitrage latency

Example cross-exchange logic:

if price_A - price_B > threshold:

execute_arbitrage()

Execution coordination becomes more complex.

4. Decentralized Finance (DeFi)

DeFi trading occurs via smart contracts rather than centralized order books.

Characteristics:

- Automated market makers (AMMs)
- On-chain transaction confirmation
- Gas fees
- Smart contract risk

Execution logic must account for:

- Slippage formula from liquidity pools
- Blockchain confirmation latency
- Transaction ordering risk

Example (conceptual AMM pricing):

$$x \cdot y = k$$

Trade size directly affects price via pool imbalance.

Impact modeling differs from traditional order books.

5. Custody and Counterparty Risk

In decentralized markets:

- Private key management
- Smart contract vulnerability
- Exchange solvency risk

Operational architecture must include:

- Secure key storage
- Withdrawal limits
- Counterparty exposure monitoring

Market access risk increases outside centralized clearing systems.

6. Latency and Infrastructure Fragmentation

Global and decentralized integration increases network complexity.

Consider:

- Geographic latency differences
- API reliability variance
- Blockchain confirmation delays

Execution timing becomes more uncertain.

Agents must incorporate latency tolerance into decision logic.

Example:

if expected_latency > threshold:

reduce_trade_size()

7. Liquidity and Market Depth Variation

Global and decentralized markets exhibit uneven liquidity.

Thin liquidity increases:

- Slippage
- Impact
- Volatility

Dynamic participation control is critical:

*max_size = participation_rate * observed_volume*

Liquidity modeling must be venue-specific.

8. Cross-Market Arbitrage and Correlation

Global integration enables:

- Cross-asset arbitrage
- Cross-venue arbitrage
- Cross-currency mispricing exploitation

However, correlations can break during stress.

Monitor:

rolling_corr(asset_A, asset_B)

Diversification assumptions must be validated continuously.

9. Risk Aggregation Across Markets

Global systems must aggregate risk centrally.

Consolidate:

- Net exposure
- Leverage
- FX exposure
- Asset correlation

Example:

portfolio_risk = calculate_global_covariance(positions)

Siloed risk management across regions creates blind spots.

Unified risk engine is essential.

10. Capital Efficiency and Allocation

Global integration increases allocation complexity.

Meta-layer must decide:

- How much capital per region
- How much per asset class
- Dynamic rebalancing rules

Example:

*allocation_region = performance_weight * risk_budget*

Allocation becomes strategic decision layer.

11. Monitoring and Governance Across Jurisdictions

Global agents require:

- Region-specific compliance logging
- Consolidated monitoring dashboards
- Multi-currency accounting
- Coordinated kill switch control

Emergency shutdown must operate across all venues simultaneously.

12. Operational Complexity vs Opportunity

Integration offers:

- Diversification
- Increased opportunity set
- Arbitrage possibilities
- Continuous trading cycles

But also increases:

- Infrastructure complexity
- Regulatory exposure
- Operational risk
- Expansion must be incremental.

Start with controlled multi-venue deployment before expanding globally.

13. Architectural Design for Global Agents

Recommended structure:

- Regional execution nodes
- Centralized risk engine
- Global allocation layer

- Unified monitoring system

Decouple:

- Strategy logic
- Venue connectivity
- Risk management

Modular architecture simplifies expansion.

Practical Global Integration Checklist

Before expanding:

- Implement currency exposure tracking.
- Test cross-venue execution reliability.
- Aggregate risk across all assets.
- Validate liquidity assumptions per market.
- Ensure region-specific compliance rules embedded.
- Simulate extreme cross-market stress.

Global expansion multiplies both opportunity and risk.

Final Principle

Autonomous trading agents are not limited by geography.

Global and decentralized integration expands opportunity sets but introduces structural complexity.

Sustainable integration requires:

- Venue-specific modeling
- Unified risk aggregation
- Robust infrastructure
- Strict governance

The future of AI trading is multi-market, multi-venue, and increasingly decentralized.

Success will belong to systems that manage fragmentation without losing control.

17.3 The Long-Term Role of Humans in AI-Driven Trading

AI trading agents can analyze faster, execute faster, and adapt faster than humans in many contexts.

- But they do not define objectives.
- They do not set ethical boundaries.
- They do not assume responsibility.

The long-term future of trading is not fully autonomous systems replacing humans. It is structured collaboration between machine efficiency and human judgment.

This section defines the enduring role of humans in AI-driven markets.

1. Humans Define Objectives, Machines Optimize

AI systems optimize toward defined reward functions.

Humans decide:

- What constitutes acceptable risk
- What drawdown tolerance is acceptable
- What capital allocation targets are appropriate
- What ethical boundaries exist

An AI agent does not understand long-term strategic intent.

It maximizes its objective function.

Humans design that objective function.

2. Strategic Direction vs Tactical Execution

Machines excel at:

- Pattern recognition
- Signal processing
- Execution timing
- Portfolio rebalancing

Humans remain stronger at:

- Strategic positioning
- Identifying structural shifts
- Interpreting macroeconomic changes
- Incorporating qualitative information

Example:

A central bank policy shift may fundamentally change regime structure before statistical models detect it.

Human oversight contextualizes data.

3. Model Governance and Oversight

Even fully autonomous systems require:

- Model validation
- Performance review
- Risk approval
- Ethical compliance

Humans must:

- Approve deployment
- Define retraining policies
- Review model drift
- Trigger emergency shutdowns

Autonomy increases the need for oversight discipline.

4. Managing Rare Events

AI systems rely on historical data.

Extreme events often fall outside historical distributions:

- Sudden regulatory bans
- Geopolitical shocks
- Exchange failures
- Structural market halts

During rare events, human judgment may override automated logic.

Example:

```
if extreme_event_flag:
manual_override()
```

Human intervention remains essential in tail scenarios.

5. Ethical Boundary Setting

AI agents can discover profitable but destabilizing behaviors.

Humans must determine:

- Acceptable participation behavior
- Market impact thresholds
- Liquidity withdrawal limits
- Risk amplification constraints

Ethical boundaries are human decisions.

Automation does not remove moral accountability.

6. Continuous System Design Evolution

Humans design:

- New strategies
- New architectures
- Improved risk frameworks
- Expanded market integration

Machines improve parameters within defined structure.

Humans redefine structure.

Long-term edge comes from system design, not just model tuning.

7. Interpreting Regime Shifts

AI can detect statistical shifts.

Humans interpret meaning.

Examples:

- Structural inflation change

- Monetary regime transition
- Geopolitical alignment shifts

Strategic repositioning often requires qualitative reasoning beyond statistical inference.

Hybrid decision frameworks outperform isolated automation.

8. Human–Machine Collaboration Model

Future trading systems likely follow layered structure:

- **Machine layer**: signal generation and execution
- **Meta layer:** adaptive allocation
- **Human layer**: governance and strategic oversight

Humans focus on:

- High-level decision-making
- Risk envelope definition
- Exceptional event response

Machines focus on execution precision and scale.

9. Reducing Emotional Bias

AI reduces:

- Fear-driven selling
- Greed-driven overexposure
- Overconfidence
- Reactionary trading

However, humans still manage capital allocation.

Human bias shifts from trading decisions to system-level decisions.

Governance frameworks must minimize bias at both levels.

10. Skill Evolution in AI-Driven Trading

The required human skill set evolves:

Less emphasis on:

- Manual trade execution

- Chart pattern interpretation

More emphasis on:

- Systems engineering
- Statistical literacy
- Risk modeling
- Infrastructure design
- Regulatory awareness

The human role shifts from trader to system architect and risk steward.

11. Accountability Remains Human

When systems fail:

- Investors hold humans accountable.
- Regulators hold humans accountable.
- Firms hold humans accountable.

AI agents do not bear responsibility.

Clear lines of accountability must exist.

Autonomous execution does not imply autonomous liability.

12. Avoiding Over-Reliance on Automation

Blind trust in AI systems is dangerous.

Humans must maintain:

- Independent risk dashboards
- Performance review routines
- Stress-testing frameworks

Healthy skepticism protects capital.

Trust should be earned through monitoring and validation.

13. Long-Term Competitive Advantage

As AI tools become widely accessible, competitive advantage shifts toward:

- Better system integration

- Better governance
- Faster adaptation
- More disciplined risk management

Humans differentiate systems by design quality.

Edge increasingly comes from structure, not just models.

14. The Future: Collaborative Intelligence

The future of trading is not:

- Human-only
- AI-only

It is collaborative intelligence.

Humans set direction and constraints.

AI executes with precision and adaptability.

Systems that combine:

- Machine efficiency
- Human judgment
- Structured governance

Will outperform both purely manual and fully unguided autonomous approaches.

Final Principle

AI trading agents will continue to grow more capable.

But markets are social systems influenced by policy, psychology, and uncertainty.

Humans remain essential for:

- Defining objectives
- Managing rare events
- Setting ethical boundaries
- Governing adaptation

The long-term role of humans in AI-driven trading is not to compete with machines.

It is to design, supervise, and take responsibility for them.

Autonomous systems extend human capability.

They do not replace human accountability.

www.ingramcontent.com/pod-product-compliance
Lightning Source LLC
LaVergne TN
LVHW060023210926
848481LV00013B/3777
* 9 7 9 8 2 3 3 0 4 4 0 0 7 *